First World War
and Army of Occupation
War Diary
France, Belgium and Germany

32 DIVISION
96 Infantry Brigade,
Brigade Machine Gun Company
24 January 1916 - 21 February 1918

WO95/2398/2

The Naval & Military Press Ltd
www.nmarchive.com
Published in association with The National Archives

Published by

The Naval & Military Press Ltd

Unit 10 Ridgewood Industrial Park,

Uckfield, East Sussex,

TN22 5QE England

Tel: +44 (0) 1825 749494

www.naval-military-press.com

www.nmarchive.com

This diary has been reprinted in facsimile from the original. Any imperfections are inevitably reproduced and the quality may fall short of modern type and cartographic standards.

© Crown Copyright
Images reproduced by permission of The National Archives, London, England, 2015.

Contents

Document type	Place/Title	Date From	Date To
Heading	WO95/2398/2		
Heading	32nd Division 96th Infy Bde. 96th Machine Gun Coy Feb 1916-Feb 1918		
Heading	96th Brigade. 32nd Division. 96th Brigade Machine Gun Company 10th February To 31st March 1916		
Heading	War Diary (Original) Of 96th Brigade Machine Gun Company From 10th Feby'1916 to 31st March '16 Volume I		
Miscellaneous			
Heading	War Diary Of 96th Brigade Machine Gun Co. From 10th Feby 16 Date of Moblization) to 31st March 1916		
War Diary	Grantham	10/02/1916	09/03/1916
War Diary	S/S "Humbcraft" Southampton	10/03/1916	10/03/1916
War Diary	Havre	11/03/1916	13/03/1916
War Diary	Bouzincourt.	15/03/1916	31/03/1916
Miscellaneous	Special Training Centre. Orders By Brig-General H.C. De la M. Hill, C. E. Commanding Machine Gun Training Centre.	08/03/1916	08/03/1916
Miscellaneous	Copies of This Order Are Issued To:		
Miscellaneous	A Form. Messages And Signals.		
Heading	96th Brigade. 32nd Division. 96th Brigade. Machine Gun Company April 1916		
Heading	War Diary Of 96th Bde. Machine Gun Company From 1st April 1916 To 30th April 1916 Volume I		
War Diary	Bouzincourt.	01/04/1916	04/04/1916
War Diary	Contay	05/04/1916	23/04/1916
War Diary	Senlis	23/04/1916	23/04/1916
War Diary	Bouzincourt	24/04/1916	24/04/1916
War Diary	Bouzincourt	24/01/1916	24/01/1916
War Diary	Aveluy	25/01/1916	30/01/1916
Heading	96th Brigade. 32nd Division. 96th Brigade Machine Gun Company May 1916		
Heading	War Diary Of 96th Bde Machine Gun Company From 1st May 1916 To 31st May 1916. Volume III		
War Diary	Aveluy	01/05/1916	06/05/1916
War Diary	Warloy	07/05/1916	16/05/1916
War Diary	Contay.	17/05/1916	28/05/1916
War Diary	Aveluy	29/05/1916	31/05/1916
Heading	96th Brigade. 32nd Division. 96th Brigade Machine Gun Company June 1916		
Heading	War Diary Of 96th Bde Machine Gun Company 1st June 1916 To 30th June 1916. Volume IV		
War Diary	Aveluy	01/06/1916	12/06/1916
War Diary	Warloy	13/06/1916	26/06/1916
War Diary	The Bluff.	27/06/1916	30/06/1916
Heading	96th Inf. Bde. 33rd Div. War Diary. 96th Machine Gun Company July 1916		
Heading	War Diary 96th Machine Gun Co. 1st July '16 To 31st July '16		
War Diary	Leavillers.	01/07/1916	14/07/1916

War Diary	Hedauville	07/07/1916	07/07/1916
War Diary	Senlis	08/07/1916	08/07/1916
War Diary	Dug-Out North of Albert	09/07/1916	11/07/1916
War Diary	Coy' H. Qs. Preston Avenue near Ovillers Post near British Front Line Opposite Ovillers.	12/07/1916	14/07/1916
War Diary	Coy. H. Qs. Preston Av.	14/07/1916	15/07/1916
War Diary	Senlis	16/07/1916	16/07/1916
War Diary	Halloy	17/07/1916	17/07/1916
War Diary	Bouquemaison	18/07/1916	18/07/1916
War Diary	Wignacourt	19/07/1916	19/07/1916
War Diary	Eps.	20/07/1916	20/07/1916
War Diary	Auchy-au-Bois	21/07/1916	25/07/1916
War Diary	Lebieuverie.	26/07/1916	28/07/1916
War Diary	Ruitz	29/07/1916	31/07/1916
Heading	Appendices. "A" "B" "C"		
Miscellaneous	IR/302 "A"	27/06/1916	27/06/1916
Miscellaneous	Operation Orders By Major H.A. Ironside.	27/06/1916	27/06/1916
Miscellaneous	Operation Orders O.C. A And B Sections.	29/06/1916	29/06/1916
Miscellaneous	96th Mach. Gun Co. Copy of Recommendation	28/07/1916	28/07/1916
Miscellaneous	Appendix "C"	15/07/1916	15/07/1916
Map	57th S.E.		
Heading	96th Brigade. 32nd Division. 96th Brigade Machine Gun Company August 1916		
Heading	War Diary 96th March. Gun Coy 1st Aug '16 To 31st August '16 Volume VI		
War Diary	Ruitz	01/08/1916	04/08/1916
War Diary	Bethune	05/08/1916	19/08/1916
War Diary	Cambrin	20/08/1916	31/08/1916
Heading	96th Brigade. 32nd Division.96th Brigade Machine Gun Company September 1916		
Heading	War Diary 96th Mach. Gun Coy. 1st Sept '16 To 30th September'16 Volume VIII		
War Diary	In The Trenches	01/09/1916	01/09/1916
War Diary	Cambrin.	02/09/1916	13/09/1916
War Diary	In The Trenches.	14/09/1916	14/09/1916
War Diary	Cambrin Bethune.	15/09/1916	30/09/1916
Heading	96th Brigade. 32nd Division. 96th Brigade Machine Gun Company October 1916		
Heading	War Diary Of 96 Machine Gun Company 1st To 31st October 1916 Vol 8		
War Diary	Cuinchy	01/10/1916	09/10/1916
War Diary	Bethune	09/10/1916	10/10/1916
War Diary	Bajus	15/10/1916	15/10/1916
War Diary	Guestreville	16/10/1916	16/10/1916
War Diary	Sarsle-Bois	17/10/1916	17/10/1916
War Diary	Orville	18/10/1916	19/10/1916
War Diary	Contay	21/10/1916	22/10/1916
War Diary	Albert	23/10/1916	23/10/1916
War Diary	Warloy	26/10/1916	26/10/1916
War Diary	Rubempre	31/10/1916	31/10/1916
Heading	96th Brigade. 32nd Division. 96th Brigade Machine Gun Company November 1916		
Heading	War Diary. 96th Machine Gun Company. From November 1st To 30th 1916		
War Diary	Rebempre	01/11/1916	18/11/1916
War Diary	Warloy	14/11/1916	14/11/1916

War Diary	Aveluy	15/11/1916	15/11/1916
War Diary	Mailly Maillet	17/11/1916	18/11/1916
War Diary	Beaumont Hamel.	19/11/1916	23/11/1916
War Diary	Mailly Maillet.	24/11/1916	24/11/1916
War Diary	Amplier.	25/11/1916	25/11/1916
War Diary	Montrelet.	26/11/1916	30/11/1916
Heading	96th Brigade. 32nd Division. 96th Brigade Machine Gun Company December 1916		
Heading	War Diary. 96 M.G.C. Vol X		
War Diary	Montrelet.	01/12/1916	31/12/1916
Heading	War Diary. 96. Machine Gun. Coy January 1917		
War Diary	Montrelet.	01/01/1917	06/01/1917
War Diary	Raincheval	07/01/1917	07/01/1917
War Diary	Bus	08/01/1917	09/01/1917
War Diary	Line. Hebuterne Sector. (South Portion.)	10/01/1917	11/01/1917
War Diary	Bus	12/01/1917	14/01/1917
War Diary	Courcelles. & Line.	15/01/1917	17/01/1917
War Diary	In The Line.	17/01/1917	20/01/1917
War Diary	Courcelles.	21/01/1917	21/01/1917
War Diary	In The Line.	22/01/1917	31/01/1917
Heading	War Diary Vol. XII 96 Machine Gun Coy. February 1917 Vol 12		
War Diary	Line Beaumont Hamel-Serre Sector	01/02/1917	15/02/1917
War Diary	Line	16/02/1917	18/02/1917
War Diary	Harponville	18/02/1917	18/02/1917
War Diary	Flesselles.	19/02/1917	19/02/1917
War Diary	Amines.	20/02/1917	20/02/1917
War Diary	Thennes.	21/02/1917	22/02/1917
War Diary	Beaucourt	23/02/1917	23/02/1917
War Diary	Warvillers.	24/02/1917	28/02/1917
Heading	War Diary. Of 96th Machine Gun Company. March 1917. Vol. 13		
Heading	War Diary. 96 Machine Gun Coy. Vol. 13 March 1917		
War Diary	Line.	01/03/1917	04/03/1917
War Diary	Beaucourt.	05/03/1917	09/03/1917
War Diary	Line	10/03/1917	18/03/1917
War Diary	Cremery	18/03/1917	18/03/1917
War Diary	Nesle & Becquencourt.	19/03/1917	19/03/1917
War Diary	Bacquencourt Offoy	20/03/1917	28/03/1917
War Diary	Toule.	29/03/1917	30/03/1917
War Diary	Germaine.	31/03/1917	31/03/1917
Operation(al) Order(s)	War Diary. Appendix I. 96 MG Coy Operation Order No. 15 Vol XIII.		
Heading	War Diary. Of 96th Machine Gun Company From 1st April 1917. To 30th April 1917 Vol 14		
War Diary	Line. Hd Qrs at Germaine.	01/04/1917	02/04/1917
War Diary	Savy Wood.	02/04/1917	04/04/1917
War Diary	Savy	05/04/1917	11/04/1917
War Diary	Foreste	12/04/1917	13/04/1917
War Diary	Line. H.Q. Francilly.	14/04/1917	14/04/1917
War Diary	Line HQ. Atilly	15/04/1917	19/04/1917
War Diary	Atilly Foreste	20/04/1917	20/04/1917
War Diary	Foreste Athies	21/04/1917	21/04/1917
War Diary	Athies	22/04/1917	30/04/1917
Heading	War Diary Of 96 Machine Gun Company May 1st 1917 To May 31st 1917 Vol XIV		

Type	Description	Start	End
War Diary	Athies.	01/05/1917	15/05/1917
War Diary	Athies-Licourt.	16/05/1917	16/05/1917
War Diary	Licourt-Rosieres	17/05/1917	17/05/1917
War Diary	Rosieres	18/05/1917	29/05/1917
War Diary	Rosieres Wiencourt	30/05/1917	30/05/1917
War Diary	Wiencourt	31/05/1917	31/05/1917
Heading	War Diary Of 96th M.G. Company Vol 15 1/6/17-30/6/17 Vol 16		
War Diary	Gillaucourt-Caestre-La Couronne	01/06/1917	01/06/1917
War Diary	La Couronne	02/06/1917	11/06/1917
War Diary	La Couronne-Le Carreau	12/06/1917	12/06/1917
War Diary	Le Carreau-Wormhoudt	13/06/1917	13/06/1917
War Diary	Wormhoudt.	14/06/1917	14/06/1917
War Diary	Wormhoudt-Uxem.	15/06/1917	15/06/1917
War Diary	Uxem.	16/06/1917	17/06/1917
War Diary	Uxem-Leffrinckhoucke-Coxyde.	18/06/1917	18/06/1917
War Diary	Coxyde (Camp "jean Bark")	19/06/1917	30/06/1917
Heading	96th Machine Gun Company Volume XVII July 1st-July 31st		
War Diary	Coxyde. (Camp Jean Bart.)	01/07/1917	05/07/1917
War Diary	HQ at Nieuport Company in the Line	06/07/1917	06/07/1917
War Diary	Coy in Line H.Q. at	07/07/1917	07/07/1917
War Diary	Nieuport.	08/07/1917	09/07/1917
War Diary	H.Q. at Farm in M3Zd.	09/07/1917	11/07/1917
War Diary	Coy in Line H.Q. at Farm in M32d.	12/07/1917	19/07/1917
War Diary	Coxyde	20/07/1917	20/07/1917
War Diary	Coxyde Bains.	20/07/1917	27/07/1917
War Diary	Bray Dunes Plage	27/07/1917	30/07/1917
War Diary	Oust Dunkerque (Camp 90)	31/07/1917	31/07/1917
Miscellaneous	96th M.G. Coy Relief Orders.	20/07/1917	20/07/1917
Miscellaneous	96th M.G. Coy Relief Orders.	30/07/1917	30/07/1917
Heading	96th MG Company War Diary August 1st-31st 1917 Vol 18		
War Diary	Oost Dunkirke	01/08/1917	03/08/1917
War Diary	In the Line StGeorges Sector	04/08/1917	09/08/1917
War Diary	In The Line	10/08/1917	19/08/1917
War Diary	Bray Dunes Plage.	20/08/1917	27/08/1917
War Diary	Coxyde.	28/08/1917	31/08/1917
Operation(al) Order(s)	96th M.G. Coy. Operation Order.	06/08/1917	06/08/1917
Miscellaneous	War Diary		
Operation(al) Order(s)	96th M.G. Company Relief Order 4	02/08/1917	02/08/1917
Operation(al) Order(s)	96th M.G. Coy. Relief Order No 21		
Heading	96th M.G. Company War Diary For September, 1917 Vol XIX		
War Diary	Australia Camp E of Coxyde	01/09/1917	06/09/1917
War Diary	Australia Camp.	07/09/1917	12/09/1917
War Diary	Company In The Line H.Q @ Nieuport M34a8.6	13/09/1917	17/09/1917
War Diary	Coy in the Line.	18/09/1917	27/09/1917
War Diary	In The Line.	28/09/1917	29/09/1917
War Diary	Australia Camp. Coxyde.	30/09/1917	30/09/1917
Operation(al) Order(s)	96th. Machine Gun Company Relief Orders No. 35	13/09/1917	13/09/1917
Operation(al) Order(s)	96th. M.G. Coy. Relief Order No. 25		
Heading	War Diary 96th M.G. Coy Vol XX October 1917		
War Diary	Coxyde (Australia Camp)	01/10/1917	04/10/1917
War Diary	Bray Dunes.	05/10/1917	24/10/1917
War Diary	Teteghem Area	25/10/1917	25/10/1917

War Diary	Eringhem Area.	26/10/1917	31/10/1917
Heading	War Diary 96th Coy. Machine Gun Corps. Vol. 21		
War Diary	Eringhem Area Map Reference France 19 SW 2nd Edition 1/20,000	01/11/1917	02/11/1917
War Diary	T 23 E	03/11/1917	07/11/1917
War Diary	Eringhem Area.	08/11/1917	10/11/1917
War Diary	Ledringhem Area	11/11/1917	12/11/1917
War Diary	Watou Area Map Reference	13/11/1917	13/11/1917
War Diary	Belgium Part of France Edition 2 1/40000	14/11/1917	14/11/1917
War Diary	27 L C 3	15/11/1917	16/11/1917
War Diary	Watou Area (School Camp)	17/11/1917	17/11/1917
War Diary	Belgium & Part of France Edition 2 1/40000	18/11/1917	18/11/1917
War Diary	27 L 3 C	18/11/1917	22/11/1917
War Diary	Dambre Camp	23/11/1917	23/11/1917
War Diary	Belgium 28 NW Edition 6A	24/11/1917	27/11/1917
War Diary	In The Line Coy H.Q. Kansas Farm (Spriet Map 1/10000)	28/11/1917	28/11/1917
War Diary	In The Line.	29/11/1917	30/11/1917
Heading	War Diary. 96 Machine Gun Company. Volume XXII		
War Diary	Line. Coy. H.Q. Kronprinz FM. (Ref. map. Spriet 1/10,000)	01/12/1917	03/12/1917
War Diary	Dambre Camp. Ref. Map Belgium 28 N.W. 1/20,000	04/12/1917	09/12/1917
War Diary	In the Line Coy H.Q. At Hubner F.M. (Ref Map. Poelcappelle) Transport At Dambre Camp	10/12/1917	10/12/1917
War Diary	Line Coy HQ at Hubner FM. (Ref map. Poelcappelle 1/11,000	11/12/1917	17/12/1917
War Diary	Line Dambre Camp. Ref map Belgium 28 N.W. 1/20,000	18/12/1917	24/12/1917
War Diary	Canal Bank.	24/12/1917	30/12/1917
War Diary	Le Hamel Clerques Ref Maps Hazebrouck 5A	30/12/1917	30/12/1917
War Diary	1/10,000 Calais. 1/100000	31/12/1917	31/12/1917
Heading	96 Machine Gun Company War Diary Volume XXIII		
War Diary	Recques Area	01/01/1918	19/01/1918
War Diary	Hospital Farm.	20/01/1918	20/01/1918
War Diary	B 19 D 2.2	20/01/1918	22/01/1918
War Diary	Canal Bank C 25 A 8.0	23/01/1918	25/01/1918
War Diary	Ambrose Camp B 10.d. Central	26/01/1918	28/01/1918
War Diary	Signal Farm 1 21.G.2.0	29/01/1918	31/01/1918
Operation(al) Order(s)	96 M.G. Coy Relief Order No. 30		
Operation(al) Order(s)	96 M.G. Coy Relief Order No. 35		
Operation(al) Order(s)	96 M.G. Coy Relief Operation Order No. 37		
Miscellaneous	96th M.G. Coy Relief Orders.	18/07/1917	18/07/1917
Heading	War Diary 96th M.G. Coy Vol No. XXIV February 1918		
War Diary	Houthulst Forest Sector	01/02/1918	07/02/1918
War Diary	Marguerite Camp	08/02/1918	10/02/1918
War Diary	Dekort Camp	11/02/1918	11/02/1918
War Diary	Houthulst Forest Sector	12/02/1918	21/02/1918

WO 95/2398/2

32ND DIVISION
96TH INFY BDE

96TH MACHINE GUN COY
FEB 1916-FEB 1918

32ND DIVISION
96TH INFY BDE

96th Brigade.

32nd Division.

96th BRIGADE MACHINE GUN COMPANY

10th FEBRUARY to 31st MARCH 1 9 1 6

96 MG
(coy)
VOL I
32nd Div

Confidential

War Diary (original)

of

96th Brigade Machine Gun Company

from 10th Feby 1916   to 31st March '16
(date of Mobilization)

Volume I

Will be rendered monthly
in future.

Army Form C. 2118.

WAR DIARY
or
INTELLIGENCE SUMMARY.
(Erase heading not required.)

Instructions regarding War Diaries and Intelligence Summaries are contained in F. S. Regs., Part II. and the Staff Manual respectively. Title pages will be prepared in manuscript.

Place	Date	Hour	Summary of Events and Information	Remarks and references to Appendices

T2134. Wt. W708—776. 500000. 4/15. Sir J. C. & S.

Army Form C. 2118.

WAR DIARY
or
INTELLIGENCE SUMMARY.
(Erase heading not required.)

Confidential.

War Diary of

96th Brigade Machine Gun Co.

From 10th Feby '16 (date of Mobilization)
to 31st March 1916.

A. Ironside
Capt
96th Brig. M. G. Co.

Army Form C. 2118.

WAR DIARY
or
INTELLIGENCE SUMMARY.
(Erase heading not required.)

Instructions regarding War Diaries and Intelligence Summaries are contained in F.S. Regs., Part II. and the Staff Manual respectively. Title pages will be prepared in manuscript.

Place	Date	Hour	Summary of Events and Information	Remarks and references to Appendices

Grantham	1916 10/2	9 p.m.	No. II Group Orders of date (Machine Gun Training Centre) No. 39/466 ordered this Company to mobilize for service Overseas. The Officers of this Company are as follows, & the Company is practically at full strength, except for one or two Specialists, i.e. Artificers, Shoeing Smiths etc.
			
			O.C. Company. Capt. H. A. Ironside.
			No. 1 Section. Lieut. R. M. Buckley
			                      2nd Lt. H. A. S. V. Eatonn
			No. 2 Section. Lieut. B. C. Perry
			                      2nd Lt. D. M. Morison
			No. 3 Section. 2nd Lt. R. W. R. Kerr-Smith
			                      " " G. S. Campbell
			No. 4 Section. " " L. Q. Castello
			                      " " J. D. Arthur
			
			Since these Officers speak French fairly (two fluently) and three speak German (two fluently), I feel, under present conditions, it will be impossible to record daily	

Army Form C. 2118.

WAR DIARY
or
INTELLIGENCE SUMMARY.
(Erase heading not required.)

Place	Date	Hour	Summary of Events and Information	Remarks and references to Appendices
Grantham	1916 10/2		9th recruits + intend to make a summary from time to time until the Company proceeds overseas.	W.S.J.
Grantham	1916 28/2	7.30	As I anticipated, the last three weeks have been so full that the writing up of the Diary would only have detracted from the efficient administration of the Company. In the meantime the Company has shot its Musketry with quite satisfactory results. In the Gunnery, Completion of No 12 Company (Mrs Grant 90°2) Mr Company was sent with a view of 119 Venier + Mrs Grant (90°2) in the course of Company of Mr Grant. 64 hits. The conditions ruling at Grantham even since my arrival on 28th Dec could not have been worse. In the first case 15000 men were sent to the M.E.T.C. without any previous experience of Machine Gun work and scarcely any Officers even than to Feed + Task after them. Consequently shall arrived. Moreover, apparently, this letter to C.O. Battalions did not call for intelligent men, or even men of good physique, & consequently I had to get rid of 50 men from my	

Army Form C. 2118.

WAR DIARY
or
INTELLIGENCE SUMMARY.
(Erase heading not required.)

Instructions regarding War Diaries and Intelligence Summaries are contained in F.S. Regs., Part II. and the Staff Manual respectively. Title pages will be prepared in manuscript.

Place	Date	Hour	Summary of Events and Information	Remarks and references to Appendices
Grantham	1916 23/3	9am 7.30	Company 150. Many of these men were physically fit but mentally deficient, one man being insane. This matter needed attention to again a marching capacity to be made – at the proper time. I delayed the training & the son of Public Morals on bringing & returning thousands of misfits to Grantham was very heavy. The conditions in the state about from discipline in every possible way. Men cannot obtain baths, stoves in huts are broken, windows broken, latrines flowing over, & very few lodgings tonight. It is therefore impossible to march the company with clean boots or get them to the Grand Eating Room without hungry things. 8 inches of mud & water. Meanwhile the W[illegible] (43) have been removed to places in a field together with the mules of 11 other Companies. There is a forest of mud in the Horse Lines and Companies officers to spend half the day stealing one another's harness & saddles, even mules.	

T.1134. Wt. W708—776. 500000. 4/15. Sir J. C. & S.

Army Form C. 2118.

WAR DIARY
or
~~INTELLIGENCE SUMMARY~~
(Erase heading not required.)

Instructions regarding War Diaries and Intelligence Summaries are contained in F. S. Regs., Part II. and the Staff Manual respectively. Title pages will be prepared in manuscript.

Place	Date	Hour	Summary of Events and Information	Remarks and references to Appendices
Yantlam	1916 20/3	7.30 am	To each Group, Supervising Officers are attached to help, but it appears rather that they are not helped but interfered with, consequently under a threat they are not expected by the Group Commanders. They are allowed to run below independently & the Group Officers Med. C.O.'s are asked to attend at the Plans at the same time. The Groups have no idea what the Instructors at Staff shows & the latter often so chose to divert details in the showing, & & Companies of Machine Gun, often contrary to the ideas of the Group itself.	[signature]
Yantlam	1916 9.3	9 am	We are ordered to present Burmese tommies, & our original number "35" is changed to 96, and we proceed to the 96th Infy Regt., & everything was ready & we were fully equipped & taken in when our men fell ill with Measles. His whole section (a grinder of the Company) his is mistaken here expires Army Signallers, the Artificers & the only Carpenter in the Company, have been ordered from	

WAR DIARY or INTELLIGENCE SUMMARY

Army Form C. 2118

Place	Date	Hour	Summary of Events and Information	Remarks and references to Appendices
Grantham	1916 9/3	9 pm	For 14 days we have had our Men + Officers 32 men from Depot Companies, all being but partially trained & some new, without 24 hours of Depot service on arrival. Further 14 men to make up our strength. The Section 102, J combined with our Section of The Company. During the last fortnight we have had almost continuous snow. On one occasion our foot lay in the Drains. The condition of the transport lines was deplorable. We are ordered to march at 3.10 am tomorrow morning to Ken Dowling South dock at front at 4.25 am, & then to leave Grantham South dock at 8.15 am.	Attached /Spec. Training Centre Orders 6/3/16 (p.63). Jul Ommitted X
5/4 Hunton pl 8 pm Southampton	1916 10/3		The Company got away 5 minutes before time & was satisfactorily entrained. The Company reached Southampton about 5 pm. Detrainment was satisfactory & Officials very helpful. 6 Officers + 45 men were detached & sent by another steamer. Consigned by the other ship our own some Mrs Dukes who saw sent to Rouen Camp.	

Army Form C. 2118.

WAR DIARY
or
~~INTELLIGENCE SUMMARY~~
(Erase heading not required.)

Instructions regarding War Diaries and Intelligence Summaries are contained in F. S. Regs., Part II. and the Staff Manual respectively. Title pages will be prepared in manuscript.

Place	Date	Hour	Summary of Events and Information	Remarks and references to Appendices
S.S. "Hunsgrove"	10/3	8 p.m.	and the 6 officers (incl. self) and 2 men safely arrived at the Ship. All Company felt the same thing.	H.Q.(?)
Southampton				
Havre	11/3	9 am	In the night on of our escorting destroyers ran into us & then might have been a very serious accident. As it was she struck me a slanting blow & anyway we kept being struck lightly. There was no damage done to us & and. The Hungrove safely arrived at Havre.	H.Q.(?)
Havre	12/3	12 noon	After handshook we proceeded to No 2 Rest Camp & went into huts. The weather being hot. The whole Company was in better able to clean itself at the at any time since its journey in December. All arrangements seem satisfactory, & everybody was satisfied.	H.Q.(?)
Havre	13/3	8 pm	The Company is ordered to leave Camp at 6 am tomorrow & entrain at Gare du M marchandis Station at 8 am	H.Q.(?)
Bourgincourt	15/3	2 pm	Entrainment was accomplished & train had men were not carry? Arms, wagons provided by R.T.O. for kitchen. They had men for an several cases to be put into covered wagons, sidings. Upon	H.Q.(?)

Army Form C. 2118.

WAR DIARY
or
INTELLIGENCE SUMMARY
(Erase heading not required.)

Place	Date	Hour	Summary of Events and Information	Remarks and references to Appendices
Bouzincourt	1916 14/3	2 pm	arrived at MARICOURT at 11 am / great difficulty was experienced in getting their limbers out, particularly as one wagon had slipped just behind a crane, & the team thereon had to be shifted before the same could use the crane again & the major. This altho' the delay'd the entrainment over one hour. The company was sent up by an officer from the 96th Inf. Brigade H.Q. & three A.S.C. wagons were known to help carry up rations etc. The company was unit to hold, & the huts provided were most acceptable. The 2nd Dimitrious Dumitius had also my Merviots provided tea at BOUZINCOURT for the men of the company who, when they came in, & were very welcome after an eight mile march and arrival at BOUZINCOURT at about 9 am. 15th March 16. held	
Bouzincourt	16/3	7 pm	Yesterday afternoon Brig. Gen. Yatman held an inspection of the company which had only had a few hours rest, & was not holding its own best, but he appeared satisfied. This morning the G.O.C. 39th Division, Major General	

WAR DIARY
or
INTELLIGENCE SUMMARY

Army Form C. 2118.

Place	Date	Hour	Summary of Events and Information	Remarks and references to Appendices
Bouzincourt	16/3	7 am	N.# Ryarff. C.B. inspected the Company with its transport & afterwards satisfied. After the inspection two sections & eight guns proceeded to AVELUY to relieve guns of the 14th Bgd. Mach. Gun Co. in the 96th Inf. Brigade Area. This line was from about THIEPVAL AVENUE (the road from AUTHUILLE to THIEPVAL) due South to about V.6.B.95 turning East to about X.1.85 then South West and thinly running slightly east to about X.7.6.50. Two guns went to the front line, from & the support line, & two behind near the road which runs from ALBERT due north to AUTHUILLE. We took over the position then occupied by the guns of the 14th Q.M.G.Co. The two guns on the front line are in gun emplacements & the men in dug outs of more or less description. Some of the 8 guns have occupied cement emplacements. All but four of the fighting limbers — the minimum transport for the 8 guns on the line — are kept at BOUZINCOURT H.Q's.	M at ½ Sd S.E. Edit II
Bouzincourt	17/3	10 pm	Both yesterday & today has been very active on the line and on front line guns in left sector (F.G.2) at about point V.6.99 Km East, since its arrival, a very hot time, seeing the gun is not in either an emplacement	

Army Form C. 2118.

WAR DIARY
~~INTELLIGENCE SUMMARY~~
(Erase heading not required.)

Instructions regarding War Diaries and Intelligence Summaries are contained in F.S. Regs., Part II. and the Staff Manual respectively. Title pages will be prepared in manuscript.

Place	Date	Hour	Summary of Events and Information	Remarks and references to Appendices
BOUZINCOURT	1916 17/3	10 pm	a Bomb-proof Dug-out. The Infantry were withdrawn from the front line on several occasions. The Sergt. in charge in the first occasion when Mrs. was done, having no orders, remained with his gun team until the officer arrived, & on finding how bad things were, withdrew the team a short distance and left only sentries at the emplacement. The 2nd Somersetshire Bombers when going out of the front line, handed the team their steel helmets which had not then been returned. The men were naturally frightened but stayed in an exceptionally bad piece of open trench, which was satisfactory, trying any and all only arrived at RAILHEAD the day before from GRANTHAM. On this part of the line the enemy threw over many Oil cans filled with high explosive. Some are thrown at least 800 yards. These guns are Trench Mortars.	[signatures]
			2nd LT. ARTHUR. J.F. sent to Field Ambulance today with Influenza.	
BOUZINCOURT	18/3	6 pm	Nothing special to report.	
"	19/3	"	Made a tour of F & I Sectors, right half of Brigade front, often field report from Section officer. Two strong emplacements in building here for our	

WAR DIARY
INTELLIGENCE SUMMARY

Army Form C. 2118.

Place	Date	Hour	Summary of Events and Information	Remarks and references to Appendices
BOUZINCOURT	19/3		6 mm guns. One at a point alt X.1.a.52 which has an excellent field of fire up the valley in an entirely & well-covered direction. The other is in the valley about 500 on the way up of the wood alt X.1.c.86. A gun at this point will sweep right up the valley, but when the Stokes comes out will have very little mission. I believe a very good position for a support gun would be formed on the rising ground about X.1.c.97.	
-"-	20/3	8 pm	Nothing to report. No enemy activity.	
-"-	21/3	7 pm	Nothing new to report.	
-"-	22/3	9 pm	Nothing to report.	
-"-	23/3	8 pm	Sections B and D are being relieved tonight by sections A & C. The relief is particularly dark and we are trying on this occasion to finish out & it is possible to take a gun & supports belonging to sections in and out of the trenches rather than have 8 guns in and simply change teams. It would be better to that to own guns but our teams are so small & are officered in every possible way that it appears to me it will be found quite impossible.	

Army Form C. 2118.

WAR DIARY
or
~~INTELLIGENCE SUMMARY~~
(Erase heading not required.)

Instructions regarding War Diaries and Intelligence Summaries are contained in F.S. Regs., Part II. and the Staff Manual respectively. Title pages will be prepared in manuscript.

Place	Date	Hour	Summary of Events and Information	Remarks and references to Appendices
BOUZINCOURT	24/3	10 p.m.	Relief took place without casualties, but although L.M. Officers & men 2 N.C.O's had been up in daytime & guides were provided it took from 7 p.m. at BOUZINCOURT, with 1 hour & ½ on road to AVELUY, until 2 a.m. before all guns were delivered. The men could not possibly carry all the necessary equipment & guns (not ammunition) without difficulty. It is unsatisfactory for Sections not to keep their own guns but the change can be made on the arrival until further men are added to gun teams. 5 men (without a single man sick or a casualty) on one gun were none enough in Peace, & is War impossible. It has been clear to every O.C. Company since he saw the "Establishment" of a Machine Gun Company. That the only works sufficient on paper. Taking 9 runks & whilst it is not sufficient when holding a trench line and if they were open fighting and ammunition had to be carried a few miles half the guns would have to be left behind unless half provided by the Brigade. Since the arrival of this Company I have to note that I have been helped by various stunnings by the Brig. Gen. Comments. All C.O. battalions help in every by every from Brig. Gun. downwards.	

WAR DIARY
~~INTELLIGENCE SUMMARY.~~
(Erase heading not required.)

Army Form C. 2118.

Place	Date	Hour	Summary of Events and Information	Remarks and references to Appendices
BOUZINCOURT	24/3	10 pm	A terrible way to my way Maryk is announced by Mr Anjork Staff. Today 4 men from each B.H.Q. of Mr Anjork have been sent to us for a fortnights course in Mr Vickers Gun. They are specially selected men & capable of learning Machine Gun Work in the minimum of time. Others will be taken & instructed later & thus are will be available of Machine Gun Companies who are not have their personnel increased. They would be miserable in field work. The Relief was made at the end of one week & reliefs will be made weekly as far as possible.	[signature]
BOUZINCOURT	26/3	6 pm	I have today arranged with 306th Batt to R.E. to put in a new Gun emplacement 20 yards rear of Mr L4 of CHOWBENT STREET (at extreme right of F&2) in front line, & then bomb-proof dug-outs 25 yards down CHOWBENT STREET to which the gun & team can go in the event of a heavy bombardment. By removing this gun 100 yards south of its present position a much better stretch of ground is covered before the hill drops away to the rear. The fire is crossed with our front line gun in F.G.I between CHEQUERBENT ST and	

Army Form C. 2118.

WAR DIARY
or
INTELLIGENCE SUMMARY.
(Erase heading not required.)

Instructions regarding War Diaries and Intelligence Summaries are contained in F.S. Regs., Part II. and the Staff Manual respectively. Title pages will be prepared in manuscript.

Place	Date	Hour	Summary of Events and Information	Remarks and references to Appendices
BOUZINCOURT	25/3	6 p.m.	BURY AVENUE, about 600 yds north. The guns refused to m. F.G.2 is at about point V.6.b.99. The guns refused to m. E.G.1 is at about point X.1.a.24.	Ref. Map 57 d S.E. 1/20000 2nd edition
BOUZINCOURT	26/3	5 p.m.	Arrangements have been concluded for machine gun by guns of my guns in cooperation with the 14th Inf. Brigade who are making a raid on enemy trenches.	
BOUZINCOURT	27/3	4 p.m.	Two guns were sent to AVELUY Yesterday afternoon from H.Q. to supplement the 2 machine guns now on the line. The instruction was ordered to march 15 minutes later. Immediately after arrival at AVELUY billet a shell (one of several) fell 5 yards behind the waggon blew in the side of a wall & wounded 4 men of an infantry batt'n. The shell was a stray one, but had it hit the waggon our section would have lost two guns, + had not the precaution been taken to march in extended fortier the instruction behind the waggon must have had several casualties. All arrangements had been made & the two guns moved up to their fire	

Army Form C. 2118.

WAR DIARY
~~INTELLIGENCE SUMMARY.~~
(Erase heading not required.)

Instructions regarding War Diaries and Intelligence Summaries are contained in F. S. Regs., Part II. and the Staff Manual respectively. Title pages will be prepared in manuscript.

Place	Date	Hour	Summary of Events and Information	Remarks and references to Appendices
BOUZINCOURT	27/3	4pm	The positions about 1500 yards behind the front line. According to orders (Section orders attached marked A) fire was to be opened on the selected point, the village of OVILLERS-LA-BOISELLE at 12 midnight onwards until the raid was carried out. Several other machine guns were firing at the same place & the object was to attack the enemy's attention away from the exact point where the raid was to be made. Three guns worked well. One gun though having a broken cartridge, mung'd up, did badly. Altogether about 10,000 rounds were fired. Unfortunately the Mine which was to be exploded was late & apparently the actual raid was unsuccessful.	APPENDIX marked 'A'
BOUZINCOURT	28/3	8pm	Nothing of importance to report. The two guns & teams went to AVELUY have returned.	[signature]
BOUZINCOURT	29/3	4pm	Nothing to report. Two Sections in BOUZINCOURT went out on field work for practice. This was the first occasion it was possible to arrange this. The work done was successful but brought out the difficulty of getting on transport anywhere near the guns in an advance and	[signature]

WAR DIARY or INTELLIGENCE SUMMARY

Army Form C. 2118.

Place	Date	Hour	Summary of Events and Information	Remarks and references to Appendices
	1916			
BOUZINCOURT	29/3	7 pm	The Battalion is inadequate personnel of a Machine Gun Company as it personnel constituted. Ball ammunition. There are not and + without a single casualty the guns could not have maintained their fire through continuous shortage of ammunition. At least 8, or preferably 10 men per gun is required. There are only just sufficient men for present work. I also want the larger number of men that I am asked to furnish by for work on emplacements. Every Many Gun is to be left to the R.E.!	[initials]
BOUZINCOURT	30/3	9 pm	Pattern of Sprint entered to report. Lt. T.F. ARTHUR returned from First Battalion.	
BOUZINCOURT	31/3	2 pm	Relief of trenches is now taking place. Guns + tripods have been left in the trenches and will be handed over to in-coming gun teams.	

[signature]
Capt.
96 Q.M.I.C.

End of War Diary to 31st March 1916.

No. (63)

Special Training Centre Orders by Brig-General
H.C. de la M.Hill, C.B. Commanding
Machine Gun Training Centre.

Head Quarters,
Grantham.
8/3/16.

764
Machine Gun Companies proceeding overseas.

Nos. 71, 72, 73, 74, 75, 76, 89, 90, 91, 95, 96, & 97 Machine Gun Companies will leave Grantham Railway Station to proceed overseas for actice service during the night of Thursday 9th. March, 1916 and Friday 10th. March 1916.

The following will be times for each Company to parade and to pass the Starting Point, and train time tables

The Starting Point will be the Office of No.2 Group, known as the Brigade office.

No.Coy.	Time of Parade.	Time to pass Starting point.	Dock at which to Entrain.	Train leaves Grantham.
71	6.45 p.m.	8 p.m.	South.	11.50 p.m.
72	7.15 p.m.	8.30.p.m.	Military.	12.30 a.m
73	8.10 p.m.	9.25 p.m.	South.	1.15 a.m.
74	8.40 p.m.	9.55 p.m.	Military.	1.55 a.m.
75	9.40 p.m.	10.55 p.m.	South.	2.45 a.m.
76	10.10 p.m.	11.25.p.m.	Military.	3.25 a.m.
89	11.10.p.m.	12.25 a.m.	South.	4.15 a.m.
90	11.25 p.m.	12. 40.a.m.	Military.	4.40 a.m.
91	12.40.a.m.	1.55 a.m.	South.	5.45 a.m.
95	1.30 a.m.	2.45.a.m.	Military.	6.45 a.m.
96	3.10.am	4.25 a.m.	South.	8.15 a.m.
97	3.30 a.m.	4.45 a.m.	Military.	8.45 a.m.

Route to be followed will be via: Brigade Office, Londonthorpe Road.

Companies Entraining at South Dock will march via, High Street, St. Peters Hill and Station Road.

No. (63)

(SHEET 2)

764 continued. Companies Entraining at the Military Dock will march via Springfield Road.

765 Refreshments. The Countess Brownlow has kindly arranged to distribute refreshments to Officers, N.C.O's and men of Machine Gun Companies proceeding overseas. For this purpose Companies will be halted as the head of each reaches a point of 50 yards short of Station Road where refreshment will be served out. ½ hour will be allowed for this halt and is not to be exceeded. No men are to be permitted to fall out and drivers will not dismount.

After refreshment Companies will proceed and will be again halted as the head of each arrives at a point of 50 yards short of the entrance to each Dock.

The Company Commander and Transport Officer will immediately report to the Entraining Officer.

766 Discipline. Officer Commanding Companies will make arrangements to prevent alcoholic drink being given to their men.

767 Entraining Officers. Capt. V.C.S. Cowley will be the Entraining Officer at South Dock.

Lt. T.E. Price will be the Entraining Officer at Military Dock.

Capt. A.L. Harrison and Capt. G.A. Rosser will respectively take over this duty at 2. a.m.

768 Meals. The Officer Commanding No. 2 Group will arrange for a hot meal for all ranks one hour before parade.

769 Horses & Mules. Horses and Mules will be watered and fed 1 hour before parade.

No. (63)

(SHEET 3)

770 Men in Readiness.

The Officer Commanding Nos. 1, 2 & 3 Groups will cause the N.C.O's and men of No. 2-12 & 16 Depot Companies and No. 100 Machine Gun Company who are detailed to be in readiness to proceed overseas to be paraded and marched to report to the Officer Commanding No. 2 Group by 6.30 p.m. One Officer per Company will be in attendance with the men of his Company and will have the Field Conduct Sheets of the party in his possession. The Officer Commanding No. 2 Group will arrange accomodation for this party (strehgth 57) and will supply food for them at 2.a.m.

771 Witnesses.

Witnesses detailed by the Chief Instructor will report to the Commander of Companies to which they are detailed ½ hour before the time of Parade.

772 Men in Readiness required to proceed.

The Adjutant No. 2 Group will be in charge of the party in readiness. He will notify Commanders of Companies where demands should be made for men required to replace casualties. All demands for men to proceed will be made to the Adjutant No. 2 Group in writing. He will despatch the ranks that may be asked for. An Officer of the Company making the demand will attend to receive these.

The Adjutant No. 2 Group will render rolls of men handed over to these Head Quarters by 11.a.m. on the 10th. inst.

773 Officers in Readiness.

The following Officers will be in readiness to replace casualties. They will report to the Adjutant No. 2 Group at the office of No.2 Group, Belton Park Camp at 6.30 p.m. 9th. March 1916, and will have all kit etc. ready to proceed. (Next of kin will be taken before proceeding.)

2/Lt. M. Cohen.   8 Depot Company.
2/Lt. A.F.E. Prescott.   9   do

No. (63)

(SHEET 4)

773 continued.	Lt. V.A.Tyler.	13 Depot Company.
	2/Lt. R.W.Lamb.	14 do
	2/Lt. N.Brampton.	16 do

774 Entraining. Entraining of Companies will be carried out in accordance with Circular Memo 20 G/$-\frac{1}{3}$0 which has been issued to all concerned.

775 G.S. Wagons. The Officer Commanding Transport Training School will detail 1 pair of horses to take the G.S.Wagon of each Company containing Officers kits etc., to the Station.

As each wagon is unloaded it will return direct to the Transport Training School.

776 Railway Warrants & Train Time Tables. Railway Warrants and Train Tables will be sent to the Adjutant No. 2 Group and will be handed by him to Company Commanders.

777 Company Commanders Reporting. Company Commanders will report to the Officer Commanding No. 2 Group at the office of that Group 5 minutes before the time of passing the Starting Point.

778 Police. The Officer Commanding No. 2 Group will arrange for 1 N.C.O and 1 man for Police duty to report to the Entraining Officer at each Dock at 9.30 p.m. A relief for these should be arranged for 2. a.m.

779 Fatigue Party. The Officer Commanding No. 5 Group will detail a Fatigue party of 2 N.CO's and 12 men with one Motor Lorry to convey tables chairs etc. from Harrowby Camp to place where refreshments are distributed, where party will report to Capt. Pettle by 7. p.m. This party will be required all night a relief should be sent at 2. a.m.

(Sgd) J.A.Clancey,
2nd. Lieut & Adjutant.
Machine Gun Training Centre.

COPIES OF THIS ORDER ARE ISUED TO:

3 Copies to General Staff.
2   "   " "M" Office.
1   "   " Quarters Master. Head Quarters.
3   "   " Administrative Staff.
2   "   " Officer Commanding all Groups.
2   "   " Each Machine Gun Company proceeding.
1   "   " No. 2,12 & 16 Depot and 100 Machine Gun Company.
1   "   " Capt. V.L.S.Cowley.
1   "   " Lieut. T.E.Price.
1   "   " Capt. A.L.Harrison.
1   "   " Capt. G.A.Rosser.
2   "   " Transport Training School.
1   "   " Adjutant. No. 2 Group.
2   "   " Chief Instructor.
2   "   " Chief Supervising Officer.
1   "   " Railway Transport Officer.
1   "   " Quarter Master No. 2 Group.
1   "   " 2nd. Lieut. M.Cohen.
1   "   " 2nd. Lieut. A.F.E.Prescott.
1   "   " Lieut. V.A.Tyler.
1   "   " 2nd. Lieut. Lamb.R.W.
1   "   " 2nd. Lieut. N.Brampton.

"A" Form.
MESSAGES AND SIGNALS.
Army Form C. 2121.

No. of Message..........

Prefix...... Code......m.	Words	Charge	This message is on a/c of:	Recd. at......m.
Office of Origin and Service Instructions.				Date..........
SECRET	Sent At......m. To...... By......		..................Service. (Signature of "Franking Officer.")	From...... By......

TO { DEVASTATION. AVELUY and EGYPT

Sender's Number	Day of Month	In reply to Number	
1R/7	26 Mar	—	AAA

MAP 57 D S.E. 20000 Operation Order.

The indirect fire to be directed upon X8 will consist of two distinct types. The operation will take place tonight at the times indicated below and will be performed by the indirect fire guns.

(a) At 12 midnight A, B and C Sections Guns will fire in conjunction with other guns. Heavy fire will be directed upon X8 but not continuous and this will last until 12.15 am. It will consist of bursts of about 100 rounds at a time. And at frequent intervals of a few minutes, i.e. one or two ~~minutes~~ minutes.

(b) At 12.15 am when the attack upon

From			
Place			
Time			

"A" Form.
MESSAGES AND SIGNALS.
Army Form C. 2121.

Prefix......... Code.........m.	Words	Charge	This message is on a/c of:	Recd. at............m.
Office of Origin and Service Instructions.				Date..................
	Sent		.................Service.	From.................
	At.............m.			
	To............			By
	By............	(Signature of "Franking Officer.")		

TO {

| Sender's Number | Day of Month | In reply to Number | |
| 1717 | 26 Mar | | AAA |

The enemy trenches is to be made,
continuous fire must be directed
without any cessation for 8 minutes
until 12.23 am.

After 12.23 am fire should slacken
according to circumstances.

A messenger from guns in both FG1
and FG2 Sectors should be left
at Battalion H.Q. with orders to bring
information in the event of an enemy
counter attack. A message should be
sent to the Adjutant with the
messenger to that effect.

The point to bear in mind when

"A" Form.
MESSAGES AND SIGNALS.
Army Form C. 2121.

Sender's Number	Day of Month	In reply to Number	AAA
1R17	26 Mar	—	

Firing from 12 midnight to 12.15 am
via MGs enough ammunition in belts
in belts and can be supplemented by
belt filling machines to ensure
continuous fire from 12.15 to 12.23 am
& if need be continue fairly heavy
fire for some time afterwards.

From **DEVASTATION**
Place
Time 4 pm

96th Brigade.

32nd Division.

96th BRIGADE MACHINE GUN COMPANY

APRIL 1 9 1 6

WAR DIARY
or
INTELLIGENCE SUMMARY.
(Erase heading not required.)

Army Form C. 2118.

Confidential

War Diary of

96th Bde Machine Gun Company

from 1st April 1916 to 30th April 1916

Volume I

O.C. 96th Bde M.G.C.

Original.

WAR DIARY
or
INTELLIGENCE SUMMARY.
(Erase heading not required.)

Army Form C. 2118.

Place	Date	Hour	Summary of Events and Information	Remarks and references to Appendices
	1916			
BOUZINCOURT	1/4	6pm	Nos 1 and 3 Sections were relieved this afternoon by Nos 2 and 4 Sections. The turn was very windy and consequently the relief was considerably delayed. It is often so in the case of reliefs by small units, as orders are not issued to other units to remain quiet, and if an shot at the enemy they usually retaliate, which is apt to be unfortunate for the relieving parties.	Reference Map of Primus Sheet 57 D SE
-do-	2/4	6pm	One gun on right of Brigade front was relieved today by 90th Bde M. Gun Co. This gun & team has returned to H.Qs.	Appx 2.
-do-	3/4	5pm	The other 7 guns on line were relieved by the 14th Bde M.G. Co in the afternoon. All very quiet. All guns now at H.Qs.	A(e)
-do-	4/4	9pm	Company moved by road from BOUZINCOURT to CONTAY via SENLIS into Billets for rest with the Brigade.	A(e)
CONTAY	5/4	6pm	Company bathed & generally cleaned up.	A(e)
-do-	6/4	6pm	Training in Machine Gun work commenced. O.C. Company directed to 2mm 1½ hours squad & rifle drill with Physical drill to commence each day.	A(e)
-do-	7+8/4	5pm	Training principally in the field by Sections, but with full transport. This work was very successful + everyone learned a great deal.	A(e)

Army Form C. 2118.

WAR DIARY
or
INTELLIGENCE SUMMARY.
(Erase heading not required.)

Instructions regarding War Diaries and Intelligence Summaries are contained in F. S. Regs., Part II. and the Staff Manual respectively. Title pages will be prepared in manuscript.

Place	Date	Hour	Summary of Events and Information	Remarks and references to Appendices
	1916			
CONTAY	9/4	9a.m.	Sunday. Church Parade & complete rest.	MEO
ditto	10/4	7p.m.	A good day in the field but ultimately spoilt by mental paralysis of two officers who having spent too long on the road concluded the performance was over & went home.	MEO
ditto	11/4	6p.m.	Training spoilt by rain.	MEO / MEO / MEO
ditto	12/4	7p.m.	ditto	
ditto	13/4	"	Transport inspected by G.O.C. in the rain. G.O.C. stated that there was great improvement since last inspection. Transport Officer is doing good work. Lt. Buckley.	MEO / MEO
ditto	14/4	8p.m.	Company football & worked in billets owing to rain.	MEO
ditto	15/4	6p.m.	G.O.C.'s Inspection of Company. Very satisfactory, could have been much better had on a two officers chosen more wisely.	MEO
ditto	16/4	7p.m.	Church Parade & Football. Yesterday afternoon the Company took part in a 3 mile Cross Country Run. Each Company from the four battalions was represented by 30 men & ran first on 20. Seventeen teams completed over	MEO

T2134. Wt. W708—776. 500000. 4/15. Sir J. C. & S.

Army Form C. 2118.

WAR DIARY
or
INTELLIGENCE SUMMARY.
(Erase heading not required.)

Instructions regarding War Diaries and Intelligence Summaries are contained in F. S. Regs., Part II. and the Staff Manual respectively. Title pages will be prepared in manuscript.

Place	Date	Hour	Summary of Events and Information	Remarks and references to Appendices
CONTAY	1916 16/4	8 p.m.	This Company ran South. Three Companies of 2nd Inniskillings came from South. 16th Yorks Pion. and fifth Inniskillings. The Company hopes to beat all the Companies of two battalions and 3 Companies of the other. This shows that our men are in pretty good condition.	
ditto.	17/4	7 p.m.	Staff Ride. Rain came down. Seem weak on fields.	
ditto.	18/4	6 p.m.	Stableman. Brigade Scheme with all Machine Guns out.	
ditto.	19/4	6 p.m.	Route march in rain + Steel Helmets with complete transport. Rain only comment when the start but gradually became worse.	
ditto.	20/4	7 p.m.	Brigade Tactical Scheme. All guns out + good work done. Arrangements have been made to bring 15 men from Battalions into the Company to replace Casualties + 12 men returned to Barr as unfit + useless. All these men have been forcibly trained by one and are of the greatest benefit to the Company, all being smart + physically fit men. This will stiffen the Company, but it does not increase the strength of the Armoured which is hopelessly weak. We will never be able to keep going in the field with such inadequate numbers which has been	

Army Form C. 2118.

WAR DIARY
or
INTELLIGENCE SUMMARY.
(Erase heading not required.)

Instructions regarding War Diaries and Intelligence Summaries are contained in F. S. Regs., Part II. and the Staff Manual respectively. Title pages will be prepared in manuscript.

Place	Date	Hour	Summary of Events and Information	Remarks and references to Appendices
CONTAY	1916 20/4		Proceed continually on our Field Days. The new German Machine Gun Company has 10 men per gun which is undoubtedly the result of their own experience. In the field 8 men per gun is essential to keep the Gun working & supply it with ammunition, and allow for small casualties. Rain. Little good work could be accomplished.	
do	21/4	8 p		
do	22/4	8 p	Sections 3 & 4 have moved to SENLIS en route for the line.	
SENLIS	23/4	8 p	Sections 3 & 4 have moved from SENLIS to AVELUY & have taken over billets from 14th Dvl. M.G. Co. The transport for these two sections has moved to BOUZINCOURT. Sections 1 & 2 and Headquarters have moved to SENLIS.	
BOUZINCOURT	24/4	8 p	Sections 3 & 4 have taken over 8 guns in the line from 97th Div. M.G. Co + Sections 1 & 2, 4 guns have gone in on the left of the line AUTHUILLE & THIEPVAL. Only one of those positions is on the front line all others being in the support line where sited for firing positions and immediately to the front of 96th Bde + are placed under my orders. Eight guns of the 97th have gone into AVELUY in reserve and attached to the	

Army Form C. 2118.

WAR DIARY
or
INTELLIGENCE SUMMARY.
(Erase heading not required.)

Instructions regarding War Diaries and Intelligence Summaries are contained in F. S. Regs., Part II. and the Staff Manual respectively. Title pages will be prepared in manuscript.

Place	Date	Hour	Summary of Events and Information	Remarks and references to Appendices
BOUZINCOURT	24/1	8.30p	Transport and 9 M. Stores were here had tomorrow I take over my quarters in AVELUY, which is nearer, the line and is also the terminus of Brigade Post on the road of trouble.	AEB
AVELUY	25/1	8p	Headquarters moved here. After a fruitly there is suspicion of the line it is clear that for two miles from the line gun to villages or units behind the line is not enough to the line & supports. Emplacements in all were complimone, & hopes enough for Brick Guns, and no war has been made of natural cover. If there 26 shrined & Trench Mortars from Officers were put on Divisional Staff it seems trench mortars and Machine Guns & Engineer Officers wanting labor & nature of material. The only emplacements which are strong are no Field of fire shown in several cases the chance of it could actually be obtained within 10 or 15 yards, & sometimes less.	AEB
AVELUY	26/1	9p	16th gen & LT KERR SMITH have gone to BOUZINCOURT & received a class for a further 16 men attached by Brigade for instruction.	AEB
do	27/1	8p	Half the guns have now set up & experimented with behind the line upon the	

Army Form C. 2118.

WAR DIARY
or
INTELLIGENCE SUMMARY.
(Erase heading not required.)

Instructions regarding War Diaries and Intelligence Summaries are contained in F. S. Regs., Part II. and the Staff Manual respectively. Title pages will be prepared in manuscript.

Place	Date	Hour	Summary of Events and Information	Remarks and references to Appendices
AVELUY	27/1	8h	Enemy Front & Support lines at works. Observation of fire has been obtained in several cases with most satisfactory results. Two German guns presumably fire from about point X 2 d 5.5 into AUTHUILLE WOOD & every return & working parties. I have decided to reply with fire from guns in very close enemy gun positions upon the front & support lines noted scale and from point X 2 a 0.0 to X 2 c 5.0. The four guns on on a curved line in trenches from W 11 d 7.2 to W 12 c 3.5. Then on the cliff in their agarden, ranters, largely through gun teams being very interested and causing a large amount of pieces of pieces & various quantities of food.	JCJ
ditto	28/1	7h	Last night an enemy M Gun fire was on duty on a gun on the support line at the time & was shot by a (spent bullet) through the neck.	JCJ
ditto	29/1	7h	Indirect fire as stated in return dated 27/1 has been quite successful. An enemy Machine Gun on very quiet & CO Batt in next brigade on right has specially asked that it be continued. 9 guns can now be	JCJ

Army Form C. 2118.

WAR DIARY
or
INTELLIGENCE SUMMARY.
(Erase heading not required.)

Place	Date	Hour	Summary of Events and Information	Remarks and references to Appendices
AVELUY	1916 29/1		Moved on to second Section at about a moments notice & Mr G.O.C is strongly in favour of continually moving the enemy's supports, lines & transport roads.	[signature]
do	30/1	7am	At about 3 am enemy on the right of our Brigade commenced a vigorous bombardment quickly turning on to our right Sector R 25 & R 31 and many Shells, Gil-cans, trench-mortars & rifle-grenades. Our artillery immediately opened & all my guns did incisive fire down the German front & support lines. Three guns had turned their rounds during the afternoon which we sent to sweep up & down "Yeomen' lane" & the enemy front line, their three guns being enfiladed from AUTHUILLE WOOD. Enemy did not attack. The front entrench trenches on front & were intense.	[signature]

[signature]
Capt
O.C. 96 Col M. S. Co.

96th Brigade.

32nd Division.

96th BRIGADE MACHINE GUN COMPANY

M A Y   1 9 1 6:

Army Form C. 2118.

96 M.G
XXII Vol 3

WAR DIARY
or
INTELLIGENCE SUMMARY.
(Erase heading not required.)

Original.

War Diary.
of
96th Bde Machine Gun Company

From 1st May 1916   To 31st May 1916.

[signature]
Major
Comdg 96 Bde M.G. Company.

VOLUME III

Army Form C. 2118.

WAR DIARY
or
INTELLIGENCE SUMMARY.
(Erase heading not required.)

Instructions regarding War Diaries and Intelligence Summaries are contained in F.S. Regs., Part II. and the Staff Manual respectively. Title pages will be prepared in manuscript.

Place	Date	Hour	Summary of Events and Information	Remarks and references to Appendices
AVELUY	May 1st	7 pm	The Company is still on the line from THIEPVAL WOOD to the NAB at point of AUTHUILLE WOOD. The guns being periodically played on the support line.	Sheet 57D SE 1/20,000
ditto	2nd	6 pm	Nothing special to report.	
ditto	3rd	7 pm	— ditto —	
ditto	4th	7 pm	— ditto —	
ditto	5th	6 pm	— ditto —	
ditto	6th	8 pm	At 12 midnight the 15th LANCS FUS. raided the enemy trenches at about point X.1.6. 2.8. in conjunction with the Artillery and Machine Guns. The arrangement was that at 12 o'clock artillery should bombard enemy line at OVILLERS-LA-BOISELLE to distract their attention, at 12.15 a heavy extreme bombardment should be opened on the THIEPVAL line so return that enemy would think this to be the relief point and that the raid should be made at 12.25 on the point stated (further south) covered by an artillery barrage & continuous Machine Gun fire. 10 of my guns were arranged for this this fire & 2 for Church in St Martin:— FIRST PHASE. 3 guns fired from about W.12.c + W.11.b. A.1 gun from X.1.a 1.2. on to German Support line about OVILLERS-LA-BOISELLE.	Sheet 57D SE 1/10,000

Army Form C. 2118.

WAR DIARY
or
INTELLIGENCE SUMMARY.
(Erase heading not required.)

Instructions regarding War Diaries and Intelligence Summaries are contained in F. S. Regs., Part II. and the Staff Manual respectively. Title pages will be prepared in manuscript.

Place	Date	Hour	Summary of Events and Information	Remarks and references to Appendices
AVELUY	May 6th	8 pm	SECOND PHASE. Guns at X1.c.1.2 ceased firing until 12.25 am; then 3 guns switched above switched around to support line in R.31; 3 guns at about N.6 central turned on to same line; and on to front line - where observation had previously been obtained by day. 1 gun at W.12.a.9.8. firing on to support line R.25 and R.31, 1 gun at X.1.c.4.8 on to same point, and 1 gun at about W.6.a.7.6. Together 9 guns. When minor bombardment of THIEPVAL SECTOR ceased at 12.24 several guns, which could do so, returned to the front line from support line to assist the trenches when they were re-manned, and 3 guns in W.12 switched off for men in galleries etc. THIRD STAGE. When raid took place the following 5 guns supported it, their arcs mark fire. One gun under 2nd LT. D.M. MORISON, with Pte THOMPSON and CORP DAVIES, went out into "No-man's-land" at about point X.1.a.8.5. & covered the left flank of the raid firing continuously at the enemy trenches which to prevent them firing at their backs. Pte THOMPSON, M.E. was slightly wounded thro'l the leg. Pte THOMPSON, M.E. was slightly wounded thro'l the leg. 2nd LT. CAMPBELL R.S. laid a gun more or less in the open at about point X.1.d.0.8 which fired continuous short fire on to German front line from X.2.05 to X.2.3.0 during the raid. After dark fitted search lys	Shot 57 DSE 25000

T2134. Wt. W708-776. 500000. 4/15. Sir J. C. & S.

WAR DIARY
or
INTELLIGENCE SUMMARY.
(Erase heading not required.)

Army Form C. 2118.

Instructions regarding War Diaries and Intelligence Summaries are contained in F. S. Regs., Part II. and the Staff Manual respectively. Title pages will be prepared in manuscript.

Place	Date	Hour	Summary of Events and Information	Remarks and references to Appendices
AVELUY.	May 6th	8 pm	men build up round the gun leaving a loop-hole through which the gun could fire; head cover, beam and corrugated iron sheets were found at dusk. This was essential to cover the place the gun was to stand, sheeted & dispersed correctly on the skyline at 1000 yards on our front line was rather slow. An aerial torpedo carried away the enemy hostile after 2000 rounds had been fired & the gun had to go out of action. It was remarkable that so long as this gun was in action no rifle or machine-gun fire built out from this part of the enemy line; but shortly after it ceased an enemy M.G. opened & made things uncomfortable for the working party who had not finally returned. One gun at X.19.1.2. returned fire on to enemy line in X.2.a. & fired in all 3000 rounds. The gun fired without incident. Bn. Head. Quarters Broker, + 2 men might say without incident. Head engendered by Storm-rifle attachment. 40000 rounds were fired. Enemy machine-guns have been very active today & this evening evidenced this has been turned on to various points close to Men village and into the village. The firing Sections have been relieved on the line by X."B". 14th Bn. M.G.C. today, two Sections returning on AVELUY and the two going L.H.A. to WARLOY when Sections returning on AVELUY and the two going to WARLOY return	

Army Form C. 2118.

WAR DIARY
or
INTELLIGENCE SUMMARY.
(Erase heading not required.)

Instructions regarding War Diaries and Intelligence Summaries are contained in F.S. Regs., Part II. and the Staff Manual respectively. Title pages will be prepared in manuscript.

Place	Date	Hour	Summary of Events and Information	Remarks and references to Appendices
AVELUY	May 6th	6pm	Headquarters in Travellers Inn. The whole Bn. not been carried out without incident. Just at the most awkward time possible, enemy commenced to shell the village with 5"9 H.E. shrapnel. Up to within ½ distance of village as it were, from enemy lines. One shell landed in the billet just killing O.C. Company there + two mules, and wounding 2 men, two mules + another horse. Relief was considerably delayed with the loss of this transport. Enemy continued shelling M.G. fire.	
WARLOY	7th	7pm	Two Sections in WARLOY had baths + general clean up + rest which was badly wanted after 12 days in the trenches + not enough men.	
WARLOY	8/11	8pm	Training but no hard work.	
ditto	12	7pm	Brigade Attack. Two sections took part	
ditto	13	4pm	Saturday. Work to half an hour.	
ditto	14	6pm	Sunday.	
ditto	15	6pm	Training	
ditto	16	1pm	C in C passed by, but rather too far from Company, who were training, for him to see.	
CONTAY	17	6pm	We had received orders that we might possibly move out to MARCH Company went into rest at CONTAY.	

Army Form C. 2118.

WAR DIARY
or
INTELLIGENCE SUMMARY.
(Erase heading not required.)

Instructions regarding War Diaries and Intelligence Summaries are contained in F.S. Regs., Part II. and the Staff Manual respectively. Title pages will be prepared in manuscript.

Place	Date	Hour	Summary of Events and Information	Remarks and references to Appendices
CONTAY	May 18	8pm	O/Mvng A. repot.	
ditto	19	3pm	4.45 March for Tactical Exercise + bivouac. F.G.C.M. on Pte BRAYSHAW H. Nº 26472 and McFALL A. Nº 8790 for sleeping on their machine gun emplacement.	
ditto	20	6f	Attack at 3am + return to billets about 6.30am.	
ditto	21	6f	Church Parade + Mount took before G.O.C. 96th Inf. Bde. CORP. DAVIES and PTE THOMPSON M.E. were presented with parchments signed by GEN. RYCROFT. C.B. 32nd DIVn for devotion to duty on the night of the Raid 5/6th and.	
ditto	22	8pm	Sentence on PTES BRAYSHAW + McFALL promulgated. 3 June P.S. Company inoculated for Para-typhoid. 48 hours rest ordered.	
ditto	23	8pm	O/Mvng ordny. Draft of 8 men arrived from Base. Lot RICKHARD exposed of rank.	
ditto	24	8pm	Many men still pretty ill. O/Mvng ordny. Vergeret.	
ditto	25/26	8pm	Lectures for officers.	
ditto	27	8pm	Firing on range. Lecture at SENLIS. Battle of LOOS.	
ditto	28	9h	Church Parade. Mount hard by Brigade before G.O.C. 96 Inf. Bde. Movement order received at 7.30pm. Return to AVELUY tomorrow morning at 8.30 am will complete Company.	
AVELUY	29	9h	Company left CONTAY at 8.30 am + proceeded via WARLOY, SENLIS + BOUZINCOURT	

WAR DIARY
or
INTELLIGENCE SUMMARY.
(Erase heading not required.)

Army Form C. 2118.

Place	Date	Hour	Summary of Events and Information	Remarks and references to Appendices
AVELUY	1916 29th	9 pm	To AVELUY. Billets near Aveluy x-roads from 14 Oth M.g. Co. & reinforcements for AVELUY DEFENCES sent with 96th Co. tonight. Tomorrow all prim works with stores, tools etc. to be taken at BOUZINCOURT with instructional tour. Relief complete 2.30 pm. Took full kit on march. Transport returns to BOUZINCOURT, except 6 mules left here for carrying out rations & ammunition.	
ditto	30th	6 am	Relief of trenches completed by 4.30 pm from 97th Co. Half 97th Coy under O.C. 96th Co. reinforces the AVELUY DEFENCES. Casualties nil.	
ditto	31st	8 pm	Second new trench has been started for Machine Gun emplacements seen near ca the line before. One new emplacement has been built & occupied at the corner of the small wood south of THIEPVAL WOOD at point Q.30.d.5.1. This improves the line in this sector very considerably.	Refn. 57a S.E. 1/20000

W.C.Tronnich
Mjr
Comdg 96 Oth M.G.Co.

96th Brigade.
32nd Division.

96th BRIGADE MACHINE GUN COMPANY

JUNE 1916

Army Form C. 2118.

96 M G Coy
Vol 4

WAR DIARY
or
INTELLIGENCE SUMMARY.
(Erase heading not required.)

War Diary
of
96th Bde Machine Gun Company

1st June 1916 to 30th June 1916.

Volume IV.

[signature]
Major
Comdg 96 Bde M.G.C.

Original

Army Form C. 2118.

WAR DIARY
or
INTELLIGENCE SUMMARY.
(Erase heading not required.)

Instructions regarding War Diaries and Intelligence Summaries are contained in F. S. Regs., Part II. and the Staff Manual respectively. Title pages will be prepared in manuscript.

Place	Date	Hour	Summary of Events and Information	Remarks and references to Appendices
AVELUY	1916 1/6	9pm	Quiet day on the line but a considerable number of shells fell round H.Q.s in Aveluy without doing any damage.	
"	2/6	8pm	Aveluy shelled. Gnr Arnold wounded.	
"	3/6	2p	Aveluy shelled at 2pm and at various times during the day.	
"	4/6	4p	"	
"	5/6		Nothing of importance	
"	6/6	7pm	Last night the 9th Dorsets raided the enemy trenches at about . This was successful & 16 prisoners were taken & many killed. 5 prisoners attempted to escape when coming across No-mans-Land & were killed. Our Machine Guns gave supporting covering fire and fired 30,000 rounds during the raid. One of our guns was taken to 2/Lt D.M. MORISON to point (PENDLEHILL STREET) (THE NAB) on to the enemy lines between and point across front. It inflicted several casualties. This gun was mounted in the open and the position was very dangerous but the gun nevertheless kept going. 2nd Lt R.S. CAMPBELL was wounded by a bullet. Luckily it was a glancing blow but he has been wounded. Today has been very quiet on the line. Aveluy has not been shelled.	

WAR DIARY
or
INTELLIGENCE SUMMARY.
(Erase heading not required.)

Army Form C. 2118

Place	Date	Hour	Summary of Events and Information	Remarks and references to Appendices
	1916			
AVELUY	7/6	7pm	Nothing doing.	
"	8/6	6p	"	
"	9/6	7p	2nd Lt. CASTELLO transferred to Intelligence Corps. In view of expected enemy raid on "Ant" front 1 gun will be used rifling 2 PENDLE HILL ST.	
"		8p	2/Lt. W.H. HOLE joined from Base. Joins "C" Section.	
"	10/6		Nil.	
"	11/6	8p	14th M.G. Co. returned half 97th Co. in Aveluy today.	
"	12/6	2p	14th M.G.Co. returning 96th Co. to in the line. Half 96th to AVELUY Road + H.Q.s to WARLOY	
WARLOY	13/6	6p		
"	14"	8p	Ditto, Ditto, of.	
"	15"	9p	Nothing of importance. Major H.A. IRONSIDE went on leave. Lt. R.M. BUCKLEY O/c Company.	
"	16/22	8p	Training, especially firing + tactical exercises.	
"	23	9p	"C" Section went into line today "D" Section to Mt "Bluff", point	
"	24/25	10p	Shooting etc. for 2 Sections in WARLOY. MAJ. H.A. IRONSIDE returned from leave.	
"			Bombardment commenced today.	
"	26	9p	H.Q.s to BOUZINCOURT. Bombardment continued.	
THE BLUFF.	27	9p	Bombardment continued.	
"			28th June. Bombardment continued. "A" + B Sections brought up from WARLOY and put into the front line. Attack planned for following morning postponed.	
"	29"/30"	9p	Bombardment with periods of great intensity continued. Attack was postponed for 48 hours. Attack with Zero hour tomorrow morning at 7.30 am.	

H.A. Ironside
Major.

96th Inf.Bde.
33rd Div.

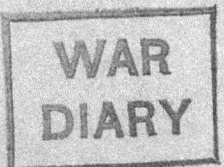

96th MACHINE GUN COMPANY.

J U L Y

1 9 1 6

Attached:

Appendices "A", "B"
& "C".

Vol 5

Confidential

War Diary

96th Machine Gun Co

1st July '16   to   31st July '16

W.H. [signature]
Major

Original

INTELLIGENCE SUMMARY

Place	Date	Hour	Summary of Events and Information	Remarks and references to Appendices
LEAVILLERS (Ruthenburg Sister Post 12 July 1916)	1916 July (?)	9 pm	When the Company went up into the line on the 25th ult: it was well understood that the attack would take place shortly, but apparently in view of the very wet & still weather prevailing, about 3 no time what was fixed for 7.30 a.m. 29th June was put off for 48 hours. This meant that the state of the Company was on the [?] two days before the attack on THIEPVAL was tremendt. & had change then period to [?] the many bombardment which were known. One a two days were spent in improvement work, drawing the bom, bomers in, but no one at this were informed. In the early hours of the morning of the 1st July '16 I had received orders from all four sections NZ M.G gun were in their assigned positions in emplacements & dug-outs adjacent to the battalions with which they had been ordered to work - as to follow - A Section 4 guns Lts CATHUR & RANKINE were to follow the 16th NORT. FUS. B " 4 " Lts PRING & MORISON C " " 4 " support " " 15th LANC. FUS. D Section 4 guns attached to the BLUFF and were ordered to eventually occupy the strong points on the Jun rds of THIEPVAL after they had been constructed. D Section 4 guns were in reserve at the BLUFF (end of BLACKHORSE BRIDGE)	Copy of orders issued to section is attached and marked A.

Place	Date	Hour	Summary of Events and Information	Remarks and references to Appendices
LEAVILLERS	July 6th	9 am	Company H.Q. with the 96th Inf Bde Hd.qurters at the BLUFF. Our line was J 10 an it's July, it includes the 16th NORT FUSt and the 15th LANC FUS1 against now the front of trenches THIEPVAL. The front held by the two battalions was as follows – 16th NORT. FUS. Southern Boundary R31 a 50.45 – R26 c 3.1. R27 c 25.75. NOrthern Boundary – line through R25 d 50.50. R25 d 40.95. R26 c 85.15. 15 LANC FUS. from left of NORT. FUS. on line through R25 b 22.62. R26 a 41.95. R20 c 85.15. On the night the NORT FUS1 fell attempt on front as they w[ent] out the jump[ing] [line]. [...] mown down by M/chine Guns, next by the time it came to the [turn of the] [...] there was nothing. I suppose no orders had been [given to] [...] there in the enemy trenches the m[...] a bridge for some reason to [...] wounded on the ground of the [...] to upset any attack they [...] att[em]pted to the [...] of the ground west the whole [...] [...] being most of the guns moved on [...] [...] [...] [...] [...] the left Bn d4 3 was J.B. Stephen followed the 15th LANC. FUS [...] at 3/10. [...] left Bn d4 3 was J.B. Stephen followed the 15th LANC. FUS [...] they had gone a few yards both officers [...] the men went down as gun was turned by a shell. The guns [...] the batteries left were destroyed by our bombers by hand firstly burned [...] [...] [...] [...] [...] [...]	

INTELLIGENCE SUMMARY
(Erase heading not required.)

Place	Date	Hour	Summary of Events and Information	Remarks and references to Appendices
LEAVILLERS	July 1916 6th	9 pm	men of the 15th LANC. FUS? could be seen in the German front line. The privates concerned he would only love the guns if he waited and actually returned to our lines safely with it. It is his opinion that had further troops been available at that moment we could have got into the north-west corner of THIEPVAL as the 9th Innisk. & Maj: J the 36th Div? on our immediate left had got well into the enemy lines & the Must. Gunn: which had covered all the approach to the 15th LANC. FUS? had apparently been put out of action. The few guns of "C" section never attempted to make for the "strong points" at the back of THIEPVAL as the enemy fire was not in our hands so those men got with shell-holes in No-mans-land at dusk ready to repel enemy counter attacks. Guns were kept in reserve. By this time the position of B & C sections in and around THIEPVAL WOOD was rather bad as all the Officers had either been killed or wounded and half of the men in "B" section as well. One gun was in No-mans-land buried by a shell. 2nd Lt J.F. ARTHUR "D" section was shaken unknown from the right and said to find out the position on the left and take charge. This he managed to satisfactorily perform. In view of the front line losses and to the fact that only 4 guns were on the right of the Bayonet Trench. Brig. Gen YATMAN, 96th Inf: Bde decided that two of the machine guns of D section should go up in support.	

1875 Wt. W593/826 1,000,000 4/15 J.B.C. & A. A.D.S.S./Forms/C. 2118.

Place	Date 1916	Hour	Summary of Events and Information	Remarks and references to Appendices
LEAVILLERS	July 6th	9 pm	Three guns were put into SKINNER ST which was quite behind the front line & a suitable point for Indirect Fire. This form of fire was largely used on the night of the 1st inst. by all Support & Reserve Guns fire being directed on to roads, crossroads & dumps behind the enemy lines.	
			On the Left Front 4 guns were put into the remains of the front line & these were kept in reserve. The bombardment was very heavy at times & there is little doubt in my own mind that had the enemy followed an intense bombardment by an Infantry Attack, my guns would have been unable to assist them, as all front line emplacements & dugouts were destroyed except one, as it was luckily the guns were all intact but there. An intense bombardment would have undoubtedly killed or wounded several men even in the already depleted gun teams. There was naturally fire infantry on the front line on the night of 1st inst. Only 17	
			The night of the 1st July was followed by a quieter day but the shelling of Support line & around Pde H.2¹ was very considerable towards evening. Orders were received for the 96th Inf Bde to be withdrawn from the front line to morrow, & in the afternoon the 107th Inf Bde came in to our left Sector, & on the night the 75th Inf Bde came in on the right B and C Section, & on the night (in the left) the 97th Inf Bde came in on the right B and C Section guns were gradually withdrawn during the night & early hours of the morning to the Château in armour, but the 73rd Inf. Bde being late in arrival	

INTELLIGENCE SUMMARY

(Erase heading not required.)

Instructions regarding War Diaries and Intelligence Summaries are contained in F.S. Regs., Part II and the Staff Manual respectively. Title Pages will be prepared in manuscript.

Place	Date 1916	Hour	Summary of Events and Information	Remarks and references to Appendices
LEAVILLERS	July 6th	10 am	and there being no sign of their Brigade Mach. Guns O.C. Company 96th Bde M.S. Co suggested to GEN. JENKINS that soon of his guns came up they would scarcely be able to turn up the trenches then filling with Infantry and in any case my guns could not get out before a further attack by 7th Inf. Bde would be launched; due for 3.15 pm. He agreed & I therefore told him my guns in his sector would remain in until relief under the arrangements on the following day & so those guns of his Bde M.S. Co would be free to follow his battalions if he wished them to do so. This was promptly attempted. 6 guns therefore moved to the 6 guns not to go forward with any advance but to help the attack if possible, & in the event of its failure to be ready to repel any counter attack. During the period of relief of the 96th Inf Bde very heavy enemy artillery fire was experienced & while the attack timed for 3.15 am was still being planned at O.C. Day-out at the BLUFF an 8" German shell burst outside the wounded, killing 27 men & officers & about 30/40 other The whole of my one autumn fellow badly wounded which added to the general difficulties of the situation. Moreover the casualties largely consisted of messengers from the 75th Bde battalions awaiting return for the attack & O'Meiren hose regiments were also killed. Sero from zero steadily been changed from 3.15am to 6.15am,	

Place	Date	Hour	Summary of Events and Information	Remarks and references to Appendices
LEAVILLERS	July 1916	10.30p 6.	Just when the men of the 2nd S. LANCS. were awakened up at 6 am it was the first they knew about the attack. They took off their packs and, it was said, though they only had to walk over to a little valley in front where there were some German M.G.'s. Actually the same thing occurred on the morning of the 1st. The 1/2 July and as soon as the men jumped over the parapet ever the Joseph German Machine Guns opened fire & mowed them down. The enemy to the immediate right of THIEPVAL AVENUE and about it were known to have their Support line and double rows to their front line. "A" Section 2nd LT. CATMUR who was with a Gun in the emplacement. Their could not however get on to them as Mod position & front it up on the ridge of the road where the first point blank at the enemy line, which was jacketed with Infantry firing at our men who were still attempting to hunt on, & upon this occurred. This plan was succesful being sniped by shrapnel & unfortunately open about 5 minutes LT. CATMUR was killed by a shell. PTE HEAD L. 7780, then jumped to the gun and PTE HUNT J. 8797 acted on 9.2 and worked the gun almost continuously between both. Then greater of an hour. HUNT was meanwhile wounded but HEAD carried on until eventually 2nd LT RANKINE came along & then being little further to do without the gun to the emplacement (sheet 5)	

Place	Date	Hour	Summary of Events and Information	Remarks and references to Appendices
LEAVILLERS	July 1916 6th	11 pm	after this LT. RANKINE was wounded. This left me with only one Officer in the line and 2nd LTS. KERR-SMITH and SIMPSON in reserve at BOUZINCOURT with LT. R.M. BUCKLEY 2nd in command. I had already sent a message back for the 2 former to join up. As soon however as they arrived, and I had given them orders, a shell burst, wounding KERR.SMITH and killing SIMPSON. This again left me with only 2 Officers. The 6 guns were left on the front line during the whole of the 3rd July, but not mounted, ready to be instantly mounted in case of an enemy attack. The bombardment was intense but not so intense as on the 1st and 2nd, and my men were killed and wounded. These guns were eventually relieved during the evening on which by the guns of the 30th Ord. Mach. Gun Co. The Company got back to BOUZINCOURT about 6 am 4th July with 15 guns (one being left buried by a shell in "No mans land"). The loss of equipment was fairly heavy as several days into the line had been blown in. One gun was also damaged but otherwise returned the DADOS in act. Ammunition etc. Casualties:	

KILLED WOUNDED MISSING (believed killed)
Officers: 2 4 0
O.R. 8 32 2

(10) Two men attached to the Company for ammunition carrying from the Brigade were also killed and wounded.

INTELLIGENCE SUMMARY

(Erase heading not required.)

Instructions regarding War Diaries and Intelligence Summaries are contained in F.S. Regs., Part II. and the Staff Manual respectively. Title Pages will be prepared in manuscript.

Place	Date 1916	Hour	Summary of Events and Information	Remarks and references to Appendices
LEAVILLERS	July 6th	11.15 p.m.	The Company acted extremely well under the most trying conditions and many acts of bravery were performed. Recommendations have been sent forward to it in hopes some recognition will eventually be obtained. 2nd Lt. H.A.F.V. CATMUR acted throughout in the most gallant manner and a copy of recommendation in his case is attached. He was unfortunately killed. Other names for special mention are as follows:— PTE CHAMBERS. A. 9°) 763. PTE HEAD. L. 9°) 780. PTE HUNT. J. 9°) 8797, CORP. PAWLEY. W. 9°) 706. 2nd LT. ARTHUR. T.F. 2nd LT. RANKINE. J.B.E. PTES HODSON. W. 9°) 10843, BARCROFT. F. 9°) 10643 (1st LANC. FUS: attached 96th Bde M. Gun Co.) Sergt BELL. R. 77)41 CORP. DAVIES. J. 9°) 811.	LT. CATMUR recommendation from attached marked "B"
	(4/7/16)		After a short rest at BOUZINCOURT where the transport was picked up, the Company proceeded to WARLOY to billets. Unfortunately during the morning a gun frightened LT. R.M. BUCKLEY'S horse which fell & rolled on him & the lost to 5th inch hospital at WARLOY. This left me with 2 Officers on being only one Officer. During the 5th July we remained at WARLOY, but proceeded (Adv'y) 6th July to LEAVILLERS.	
HEDAUVILLE	7/7/16	8 a.m.	Moved from LEAVILLERS to HEDAUVILLE.	

INTELLIGENCE SUMMARY

(Erase heading not required.)

Instructions regarding War Diaries and Intelligence Summaries are contained in F.S. Regs., Part II. and the Staff Manual respectively. Title Pages will be prepared in manuscript.

Place	Date 1916	Hour	Summary of Events and Information	Remarks and references to Appendices
SENLIS	July 8	8 pm	Moved to SENLIS.	
Dugouts north of ALBERT	9th	10 pm	Moved to dug-outs between BOUZINCOURT and ALBERT. Transport has remained at a farm half way between SENLIS/BOUZINCOURT.	
"	10th/11th	6 Am	Rested.	
Log H.2. PRESTON AVENUE near OVILLERS POST near Ovillers front line Ovillers	12th	10 pm	Relieved 14th Oct M.G.C. in the line in OVILLERS this afternoon. 7.9 am in OVILLERS (now occupied partly by British) 3 Bn/15 St. 3 DOWNST ST for indivd front and 3 in reserve without men to work them. Relief completed without casualties.	
Ovillers	13th	6 pm	A bomb attack was made last night on enemy trenches in OVILLERS by the 2nd SOUTH LANC. REGT. A trench was taken but at about 8.30 am the enemy were seen to be gathering for a counter-attack from the rear and as VICKERS GUNS were mounted 2 guns went to Point 77 & fired fire over the Shelter Moritz & scattered the enemy in JOVILLERS. The enemy were seen now & then in small numbers & fire was opened upon them but they showed no desire to come on	
ditto	14th	7 am	Last night the 2nd Denshire High & 17th H.L.I. took a further line of trenches to the north in OVILLERS and in the early hour of this morning the enemy counter-attacked & the CO of the 17th H.L.I. asked for a Vickers Gun to go up on the left. Corl. DAVIES of B Section went forward with Corl. RENNER and the gun was put in a sap running out from the old German front line, and covered the enemy lines & the parapet. Several parties of the enemy came along the parapet tending our men out of the captured trench & more of them were accounted for. Eventually a party	

67 H 25 PRESTON AV.	14th July 7 pm	2 guns were made for the 9 gun. There were killed and one managed to throw his bomb but it hastily went too far. Our Infantry however now retired to their old line. The gun was got away but the dugout was lost. The gun had fired 750 rounds. During the same affair another gun did excellent work several times getting in enfilade fire at enemy parties of 40 to 60 men all of whom never managed to get across their own barbed wire. The enemy on several occasions stormed a down to within 10 yds.
—ditto—		2 blank attacks from No-mans Land. Soi-mai 2nd LTS arrived for the Company from M. Guns Bn, namely PARSONS, RIEG, WALKER, HENRY, NEILSON, ELIAS. Pte. J. Syme went over to Bn with the BUCKLEY. We are to be relieved tonight by the M. Guns of the 144th O.R. Mar. Gun Co. LT P.M. BUCKLEY.
	15th July 5 pm	rejoined the Company from Hospital WARLOY.
SENLIS	16th July 4 pm	The retirement last night was more difficult but the Company got out without casualties or actually any equipment. 2 casualties during the four days. When coming out last night the enemy dropped large numbers of gas-shells round about and made Helmets hard to be worn. In the dark without all our transport mining made matters extraordinarily difficult. An aeroplane also flew over dropping flares & bombs, while the enemy continued shelling all roads continuously. A considerable amount of equipment was lost under these trying circumstances, but although many people were about, some thousands lying, no man in the company was badly affected or any was completely without a single casualty. We returned to billets at SENLIS
HALLOY	17th July 6 pm	March via train from SENLIS to HALLOY.
BOURQUEMAISON	18th July 2 pm	March in two relays from HALLOY.
WIGNACOURT	19th July 5 pm	March in two relays.
EPS	20th July 6 pm	March in two relays.
AUCHY-au-BOIS	21st July 5 pm	March in two relays.

INTELLIGENCE SUMMARY

(Erase heading not required.)

Instructions regarding War Diaries and Intelligence Summaries are contained in F. S. Regs., Part II and the Staff Manual respectively. Title Pages will be prepared in manuscript.

Place	Date 1916	Hour	Summary of Events and Information	Remarks and references to Appendices
ACHY-au-BOIS	July 22	6 pm	Rested. Half Section + 2 guns with LT. PARSONS went to Divisional School FERFAY.	
ditto	23	4 pm	ditto	
ditto	24/25	6 pm	Rested + refitted	
LEBIEUVERIE	26	"	Moved on limbers today.	
"	27	"	Rested	
"	28	"	Pistol work with guns.	
RUITZ	29	5 pm	Moved on bus today.	
"	30	8 pm	Rested. Sunday. O.C. Coy went + saw Support line HULLOCH - LOOS.	
"	31	4 pm	Clean up + drill.	

WH French
Major
Cmdg 96th M. Gun. Co.

31.7.16

A P P E N D I C E S

"A"
"B"
"C"

SECRET.   W.I.   "A"
IR/302   27/6/16.

The 4 Sections will move tomorrow as
follows:—
A Section will leave WARLOY at 8.30 a.m.
  and will proceed via SENLIS; BOUZINCOURT;
  NORTHUMBERLAND AV; PIONEER RD; HAMEL RD;
  to BLACK HORSE BRIDGE, and are to be in
  positions as detailed by 3 p.m.
B Section will also proceed at the same hour,
  and by the same route.
Usual precautions regarding intervals on the
road will be observed.

          A Section.

The guns will take up the following positions
unless other arrangements have to be made
later:—
  1 Gun   Top of THIEPVAL AV.
  1 "   SEMMEL TRENCH.
  1 "   AUTHUILLE BARRIER (Left of Road)
  1 "   "   "
           (about 15/20 yds down slope to left).
One guide for SEMMEL TRENCH will
be at the BLUFF at 1.30 p.m. Other
guides will be unnecessary.

IR/302   27/6/16.

② .

B Section.

1 Gun at WHITCHURCH ST.
3 " " in Emplacements and dug-outs at
            CATERPILLAR WD.
One guide will meet the team for WHITCHURCH ST.
at CATERPILLAR WD at 1.30 p.m.

C Section.

The guns of this section will come back to the
following points :—
   1 Gun to MAJ. GEN. EMPLACEMENT.
   1 " " STORE DUG-OUT (BLUFF).
   2 " " good Dug-outs ("   ).
C Section will send 1 guide from WHITCHURCH ST.
to meet incoming team at CATERPILLAR WD. at
1.30 p.m.; and 1 guide from SEMMEL TRENCH
to BLUFF at 1.30 p.m. to meet incoming teams.

D Section.

The guns of this section will come back to
the following points :—
   1 Gun to old Dug-out (BLUFF).
   2 " " big   "   (").
   1 " " in Officers " (").

③

IR/30.2   27/6/16.

D Section will send 1 guide to CATERPILLAR WD at 2 p.m. (AHQ to direct C Section gun team to MAJ. GEN. EMPLACEMENT.

2/LT. ARTHUR will show 2/LT. HOLE the exact position of the various Dugouts as detailed above. 2/LT. HOLE will see 2/LT. ARTHUR at the BLUFF before start to-day.

The greatest care must be taken not to crowd gun teams into Communication trenches in view of possible enemy activity.

Immediate reports of occupation of new points must be made to 96th M.G.Co. H.Q., which from tomorrow afternoon will be at BRIGADE HEADQUARTERS. These Headquarters will be at the BLUFF until after the move.

When these orders have been carried out they must be burned.

Copies issued to A.B.C. + D Sections.
           Transport.

IR/303.   27/3/16.

Operation Order
by
MAJOR H.A. IRONSIDE.

1. In continuation of IR/302 & all O.C.'s section will keep close touch with B'S O.C.'s. all whom they will look to work when the advance begins.

2. They will act in orders with O.C B'n. as to "jump" and obtain ZERO TIME from the same source.

In case officially should be found by unemployed to pass on this vital information.

3. O.C. Sections must decide in advance and give definite indication to N.C.O's a/c guns, at what time and by what communication sections to guns will move forward behind their respective Bn.

4. **BELT-FILLING POSITIONS.**

A Section will have one machine fixed in the emplacement at the top of THIEPVAL AV. and the other in any available dug-out close by, known to all.

B Section will have the two machines if possible, in the WHITCHURCH ST. emplacement and dug-out.

C Section will eventually occupy the emplacement and dug-out at the corner of CATERPILLAR WD., for this belt-filling machine, which on initial entry into & the assault, attack our initial into

1R/303   ②   27/6/16.

strong points which their guns will occupy
after they gain their objective.

D Section, although in Reserve and likely to be moved
in any direction, must have their machines
fixed up on the BLUFF dug-outs.

Should they move eventually, the belt-filling
machines should be moved forward if possible,
to a point as close as O.C. Section is able
to arrange.

5.   THE ADVANCE

This will be carried out by all Sections on the
lines of the manoeuvres which took place from
time to time behind the lines:—

A Section with 16th NORTH. FUS.
B   "   "   15th LANCS. FUS.
C   "   "   16th LANCS. FUS.
D Section will be in Reserve, and will
   not move until ordered by the
   Brigade or O.C. Coy.

IR/303.
G.

(3)

27/6/16.

STRONG POINTS.

A Section will occupy no strong points.

B Section will eventually occupy two strong points on the 2nd Main Objective, which are to be constructed by a Company of the 2ND INNISKILLING FUS.

They will, however, follow the 15th LANCS. FUS. when they advance, and help to consolidate the 2nd Objective by a system of cross-fire until the strong points are ready. O.C. sections must detail 2 guns for the points.

The two points will be at :—

R 26 b 8/5
R 20 d 0/0.;

approximately at the right and left of the Bn. front. 15th LANCS. FUS.

C Section will follow C Coy, 16th LANCS. FUS., and all 4 guns must be detailed by O.C. Section to the following 4 strong points, which that Bn. is ordered to construct :—

R 26 c 3/4
R 26 c 8/7
R 26 a 1/3
R 25 b 9/8.

It is of vital importance that guns understand their orders, and no gun must deviate from its particular objective.

1R/308   (4).   27/6/16.

Particularly guns for strong points must be sure they are at the right place. 'B' guns, if delayed, must not be persuaded to remain behind for occupation of "C" strong points.

6. There are no further strong points than the 6 mentioned above which are to be occupied by the guns of this Company.

AMMUNITION DUMPS (ADVANCED).

7. A B and C Sections will each carry 4 dump flags as they advance. They must be rolled, and inconspicuous. When placed at various suitable points, care must be taken that they are out of view of the enemy, both in front and on the flanks. The first flag should in no case be placed nearer the belt-filling machines than the enemy front line trenches. A line of flag dumps should, as far as possible, be formed, but any section may use ammunition at a dump even if belonging to another section. Ammunition is common to all. C Section might increase the line of ammunition dumps started by 'A' and 'B', who will have already gone forward. There will be only 2 lines of dump flags.

(5).

IR/303.   27/6/16.

The system of ammunition dumps should be thoroughly explained to D Section, so that the men may know where to look for Ammunition, whether they are eventually sent to the left or right. D Section will not carry flags.

On the last field operation there appeared to be doubt in the minds of some men as to the use of the flags. They are points which will be used by a line of ammunition-carriers which O.C. Section will arrange to have behind him; formed from his Ammunition-carriers who, (having carried up their first ammunition to the guns) will return for more, each man carrying boxes along the chain of flags. If, eventually pack-animals with ammunition are able to come forward, they will also deposit their boxes at the dump flags.

Men must not crowd at ammunition dumps, and boxes must not be dumped, and left, at the first points on the chain. The whole object is to ensure that the ammunition is certain to go forward quickly to the guns.

1R/303.   (6).   27/6/16.

8. RATIONS and WATER.

O.C. Sections are responsible that all their men go forward with full water-bottles, and rations as already detailed.

9. GENERAL.

No papers or orders are to be carried forward by Officers or men. They must be destroyed. Officers may carry the 1/20,000 trench map, showing German Trenches only, the 1/40,000 sheets 57d, 57e, and LENS sheet 1/100,000 series.

Messages and reports will only refer to these maps.

Messages must be sent back, and estimated number of Casualties in section until message is sent off, from time operation commences. This must in any case be sent back every few hours. O.C. Company's address will be

W.1. care S.A.

When possible, use should be made of Bn Messengers, who all wear an armlet with an "M" in red.

IR/303.   27/6/16.

Wounded.
Men must not fall out to bring back wounded. If "No 1" is a casualty, the 1st AID CASE which he carries must on no account be left with him, but must be taken on by the new "No 1".

GRAND COURT.
Particular attention should be given to this plan, and R.15.a. on the night of the assault, but with reference to the general situation.

LUMINOUS DISCS may be found useful for keeping direction after dark.

Do not forget that guns must be cleaned and oiled.

Scout discs will be used.

The above orders are long, and must be read carefully and re-read carefully and finally destroyed. The men must be told everything which will help them to understand the operation.

It goes without saying that the Company will do well, and I trust that the luck of the company will go with both officers and men.

———

1R/304.

W.1.

29/6/16.

Operation Orders

O.C. A and B Sections.

Original "Z" day has become "Y1" day.
June 30th " " " "Y2" "
July 1st " " " "Z" "

C and D Sections have been ordered to come up from BOUZINCOURT to be in their positions as detailed by Operation Orders 1R/302 of 27/6/16. The guns and teams of your sections will take up their allotted positions under same orders during the course of the afternoon (abt. 8 p.m.).

Teams must be instructed that at that hour they must consider they are at the same period and ready to advance on the same lines laid down in Operation Order 1R/303, as though no waiting period had intervened.

Please inform when you are complete — positions of belt-filling machines.

———

96th Mach. Gun Co.

"B"

28.7.16.

Copy of Recommendation.

2nd LT. H.A.F.V. CATMUR.

This officer acted with the utmost gallantry throughout the fighting 1/3rd July '16.

(a) On the night of 1st July he went out into "No-man-land" and searched for wounded men of the 16th NORTH FUS^{rs} for 2 hours under fire, eventually finding & bringing in a severely wounded private.

During the day & night he attended to scores of wounded.

(b) On the morning of 3rd July during the unsuccessful attack of the 2nd SOUTH LANC. REGT he went out to the barbed wire with his servant under intense fire, & after disentangling a wounded officer, "tall & thin" brought him in safely. This took between 5 & 10 minutes to accomplish, in broad daylight.

(c) Shortly after, seeing enemy infantry cross

2

from the Support line at the top & right of THIEPVAL AVENUE to their front line he got the gun out of the emplacement at the top of the AVENUE (which could only fire left) mounted it in the open on the ridge of the road and swept the German line which was packed with enemy infantry firing at the 2nd SOUTH LANCS, who were still attempting to advance, & upon our wounded.

After about 5 or 7 minutes he was killed by a shell. During the time he was firing the spot which was entirely exposed was being swept by shrapnel.

His gallant example led to others following his example & the gun was continuously worked from this position for upwards of one hour.

A.A. Fromich
Major
Comdg 96 Mach. Gun Co.

INTELLIGENCE SUMMARY

APPENDIX "C"

Extract of Remarks by Maj. Gen. W.H. RYCROFT, C.B. C.M.G.

15th July '16.

"The Division is no weaker from the Battle to refit. Since July 1st it was been almost incessantly engaged in fighting.

It has on all occasions shown the same offensive spirit without which victory cannot be attained.

The loss of brave comrades is mourned but they have not died down their lives in vain.

There are upto & down in every battle, & strong & admirably made attacks in any line. All ground gained has been held.

The THIEPVAL salient, the object of the Div'n on the initial attack, has been proved to be the strongest period in the enemy's carefully prepared fortifications line."

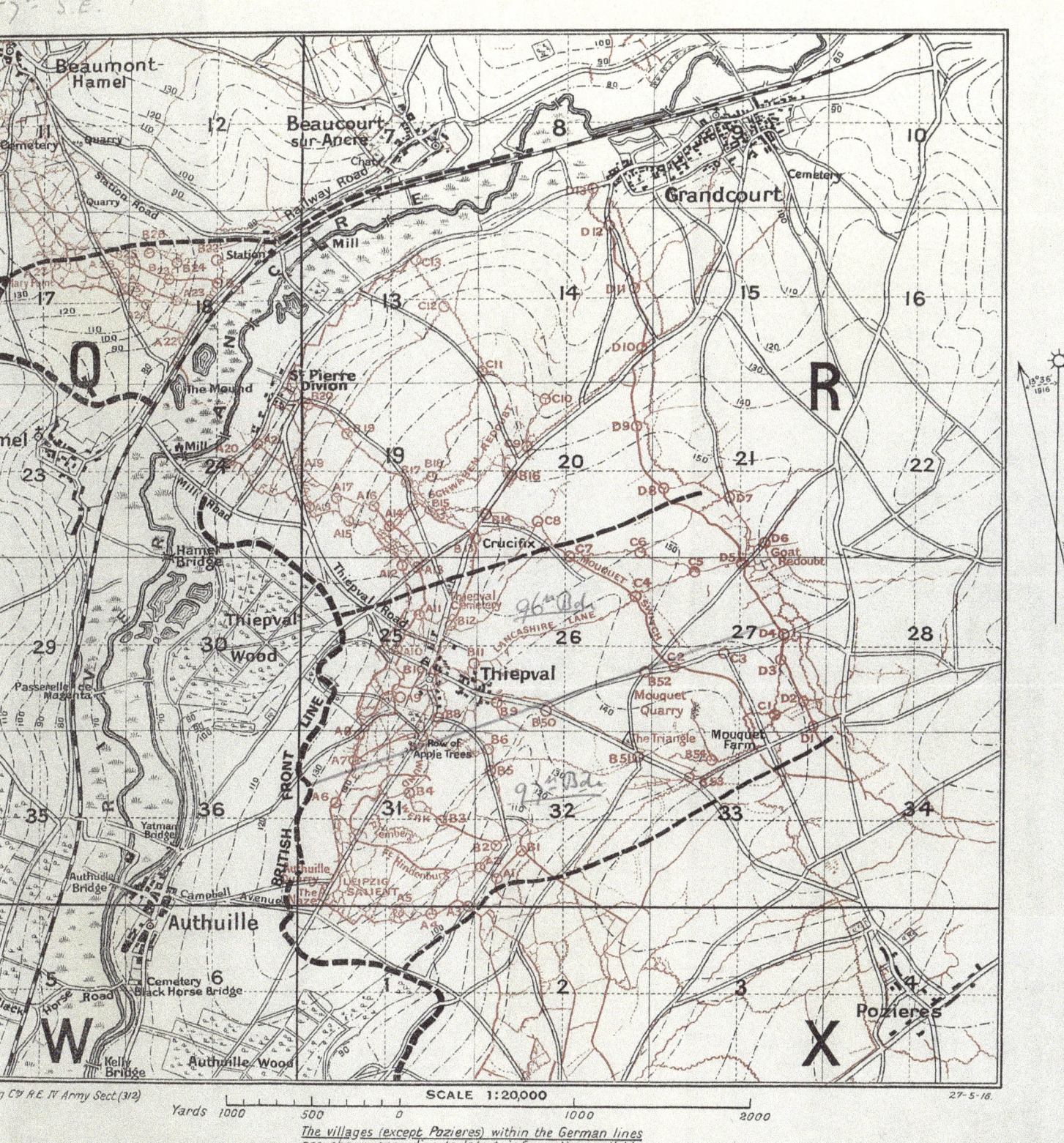

96th Brigade.

32nd Division.

96th BRIGADE MACHINE GUN COMPANY

AUGUST 1 9 1 6

Army Form C. 2118.

VOL 6

WAR DIARY
or
INTELLIGENCE SUMMARY
(Erase heading not required.)

Confidential

War Diary

96th Mach. Gun Coy

1st Aug '16   to   31st August '16

[signature]
Major
Comdg 96th M.G. Co.

Volume II

Original

WAR DIARY
or
INTELLIGENCE SUMMARY
(Erase heading not required.)

Instructions regarding War Diaries and Intelligence Summaries are contained in F. S. Regs., Part II and the Staff Manual respectively. Title Pages will be prepared in manuscript.

Place	Date 1916	Hour	Summary of Events and Information	Remarks and references to Appendices
RUITZ	Aug 1st/2nd	7pm	Resting & refitting.	
– ditto –	3rd	6pm	Yesterday O.C. Company went to LOOS and made arrangements to relieve & gave 2pm 14th Bn. M.G.C. there. This is being carried out today and half transport will return to NOEUX-LES-MINES. B & C Sections have been detailed.	
– ditto –	4th	5pm	Relief was completed last evening at LOOS but the teams are not mounted on arrival as the village is at least 2 miles of communication trenches from PHILOSOF. The weather was abnormally hot. One gun & team of D Section sent to LAPAGNOY on aeroplane duty.	
BETHUNE – ditto –	5th	9pm	We came into BETHUNE this afternoon to work and billets.	
– ditto –	6th	4pm	Saturday. Church Parade & attendance of 1st Army Tournament on GRAND PLACE BETHUNE. Several thousand troops present. L/c JOHNS and Pte HOOLEY slightly gassed & to hospital in LOOS road. Recalled by gas shell.	
– ditto –	7th	8pm	The GRAND PLACE was shelled today with 15 air H round? several huts being destroyed. Much damage & loss of life particularly to civilians. BETHUNE has not been shelled since Nov? November.	
– ditto –	8/12th	6pm	Refitting & training.	
– ditto –	13th	8pm	Returned shelled with 5·9 round the Station & main billets.	
– ditto –	14/15th	9pm	Refitting & training. 6 remaining guns go tomorrow to CAMBRIN SECTOR	
CAMBRIN	20th	10pm	6 guns came in today. H.Q. in FACTORY TRENCH, east of CHURCH.	
– ditto –	21st	6pm	1 gun from LAPAGNOY relieved by 55th M.G. Co. Half transport to BEUVRY. LAPAGNOY gun to BEUVRY for the night.	

WAR DIARY
or
INTELLIGENCE SUMMARY

(Erase heading not required.)

Place	Date	Hour	Summary of Events and Information	Remarks and references to Appendices
CAMBRIN.	22	6 p.	LAPUGNOY guns & lorries came and the trenches today relieving a further gun of the 97th M.G.C.	
ditto	23	5 p.	The 8 guns in LOOS are being relieved tonight and come to ANNEQUIN. Transport for these 2 sections will also now go to BEUVRY. Then 8 guns are to come into the line on the 25th inst. There seems are being worked too hard during past no not seeing the fighting on the SOMME.	
ditto	24	6 p.m.	Relief was carried out at LOOS satisfactorily without casualty. Unfortunately PTE HODGSON W. attached from 1st LANC FUS. died of hand failure when the relief was in progress. HODSON was a very good man & has been recommended for bravery when he brought LT. PRING in mortally wounded from No man's land on the 17th July under heavy fire.	
ditto	25	7 p.	"C" Section 4 guns took over positions from the 97th T.O. in the line & "B" Section relieved the other 4 guns of the same log at ANNEQUIN. There are now 12 guns. Yesterday it appears PTE CAPPER. T.R. received a self-inflicted wound in the right hand. This man is one of a new draft received coming the fighting on the SOMME.	
ditto	26/28	9 p.	Nothing of importance. Lewis guid. Material fire carried on nightly. 2nd LT. HENRY sent to Hospital with trench fever.	
ditto	29/31	10 p.m.	Nothing of importance. After a little storm on 30th weather almost unfavorable.	

Lewis
96th M.S.C.

H.G.Howitt
96th M.S.C.

96th Brigade.

32nd Division.

96th BRIGADE MACHINE GUN COMPANY

SEPTEMBER 1 9 1 6

WAR DIARY
or
INTELLIGENCE SUMMARY

Vol 7

Confidential

War Diary
96th Mach. Gun Coy.

1st Sept '16 to 30th September '16

W.A. Ironside
Major
Comdg 96th M.G.Coy.

Volume VII.

Original

WAR DIARY
or
INTELLIGENCE SUMMARY
(Erase heading not required.)

Instructions regarding War Diaries and Intelligence Summaries are contained in F. S. Regs., Part II. and the Staff Manual respectively. Title Pages will be prepared in manuscript.

Army Form C. 2118.

Place	Date	Hour	Summary of Events and Information	Remarks and references to Appendices
In the trenches CAMBRIN	1 Sept	10 pm	The Company still remains in the Line.	
ditto	2 Sept	6 pm	Last night all B Lewis's Guns Guns opened fire simultaneously at 9 pm & again at 9.25 pm upon the cross roads AUCHY point A 29 & 15.95. slowly traversing to the cross roads A 29 & 15. then vertically onwards the CHURCH at HAISNES, from A 30 & 50.35. A few guns were able to reach the latter point. Fire was maintained for 5 minutes in each case. Enemy appeared to be unlocated.	Map. ref. 1/20000 36 c NE Ed. 7b.
ditto	3rd Sept 1 pm		2nd LT. J.F. ARTHUR appointed to be i/charge of all Lewis's Gun guns in the Line.	
ditto	6/8 =	6 pm	Nothing of importance & no casualties. Brigade relieved fire on AUCHY & on HAISNES ROAD and other points.	
ditto	9th	5 am	Last night a raid was attempted by the 16th LANC. FUS's but failed. Our guns are rather too close to the front line to be of much benefit in these raids.	
ditto	10/11	6 pm	Nothing of importance, casualties nil	
ditto	12th	7 am	Successful raid was carried out last night by 16th LANC. FUS's. Our guns fire heavy bursts of rishfield fire over the spot where the party was to J" and in order to over the noise. This was considered successful. At 5.30 all our guns opened & swept another part of the enemy trenches in order to draw attention away from the real point. 5 prisoners taken & many retaliation small.	
ditto	15th	6 pm	4. O.R. arrived as a draft from 94th m.5.l. Apparently there are many who they want to get over to.	

INTELLIGENCE SUMMARY
or
(Erase heading not required.)

Instructions regarding War Diaries and Intelligence Summaries are contained in F.S. Regs., Part II. and the Staff Manual respectively. Title Pages will be prepared in manuscript.

Place	Date	Hour	Summary of Events and Information	Remarks and references to Appendices
In the trenches	14 Sept	5/h	Nothing of importance.	
CAMBRIN BETHUNE	15 Sept	9 pm	Company relieved today without casualty by the 14th M.G. Co. The Company was 26 days in the trenches without a single casualty.	
ditto	16 Sept	6 pm	Rest + baths	
ditto	17 Sept	8 pm	2nd Lt. COLE arrived from Base.	
ditto	19 Sept	6 pm	2nd Lt. ALDERSON arrived from Base.	
ditto	20th	5 pm	Sergts M/G SHERWOOD on leave.	
ditto	21st	10 pm	Nothing of importance. Men had further hot baths.	
ditto	23rd	6 pm	1 O.R. from Base and 2 O.R's from 94th M.G. Co. The latter unclear.	
LE PREOL	25th	9 pm	Company today relieved the 9th M.G. Co. in the CUINCHY Sector + BRICKSTACKS	
ditto	27th	6 pm	2/Lt J.F. ARTHUR on leave. PTE HARRIS No 42307 wounded at BRICKSTACKS	
ditto	28th	5 pm	Authority for 2/Lt R.F. WALKER to return to Base for further instruction.	
ditto	29th	4 pm	Nothing of importance on the line. 9 new guns are now out for further instruction.	
ditto	30th	1 pm	Nothing of further importance.	

[signature]
Major
Comdg 76th M.G. Co.

96th Brigade.

32nd Division.

96th BRIGADE MACHINE GUN COMPANY

OCTOBER 1 9 1 6

Vol 8

War Diary
- of -
96 Machine Gun Company

1st to 31st October 1916

Vol 8

Army Form C. 2118.

WAR DIARY
or
INTELLIGENCE SUMMARY

(Erase heading not required.)

October 1916

Place	Date	Hour	Summary of Events and Information	Remarks and references to Appendices
CUINCHY	1–9th		In the line – Brickstacks. Generally speaking, some considerable trouble from heavy minenwerfers.	Ref Map LENS 11. HW
BETHUNE	9th		Relieved by 2/5th & 1/9th M.G. Coys. Went into Billets.	HW
	10th		Temporary Command of Coy. taken over by Lieut R.M. BUCKLEY.	HW
BAJUS	15th		Marched from BETHUNE. Maj IRONSIDE O.C. Coy. died at BETHUNE	HW
GUESTREVILLE	16th		Marched from BAJUS.	HW
SARSLE-BOIS	17th		Marched from GUESTREVILLE.	HW
ORVILLE	18th		Marched from SARSLE-BOIS. Lieut H.F.L. WILLIAMS appointed command Coy	HW
	19th		Orders to move forward cancelled	HW
CONTAY	21st		Marched from ORVILLE. Lieut BUCKLEY appointed O.C. 166th M.G. Coy	HW
	22nd		O.C. up to POZIÈRES reconnoitre line	HW
ALBERT	23rd		Marched from CONTAY – Bivouacs Brickfields area. Weather very bad. Heavy rain. Ground very muddy. 2nd Lieut D.M. COLE to Hospital	HW
WARLOY	26th		Marched into billets from ALBERT.	HW
RUBEMPRÉ	31st		Marched from WARLOY.	HW

H.F. Williams M.G. Coy
Comdg 166 M.G. Coy

96th Brigade.

32nd Division.

96th BRIGADE MACHINE GUN COMPANY

NOVEMBER 1 9 1 6

WAR DIARY.

96th MACHINE GUN COMPANY.

From November 1st to 30th 1916.

WAR DIARY or INTELLIGENCE SUMMARY

Army Form C. 2118

NOVEMBER 1916

Page 1

Place	Date	Hour	Summary of Events and Information	Remarks and references to Appendices
REBEMPRE	NOV 1	10AM	2Lt. A.V. Parker joined Company. Brigade Field Scheme. Reference Map 1/40,000. 57 D. T. Square 14. 15. 20 + 21.	
	2		3" Billets with heavy rains. 2Lt WALNER to A.S.E. HARVE auth QMG. GHQ.	
	3	9.30AM	Repetition of Field Scheme practised on Nov. 1st.	
	4	10AM	Field scheme on a Brigade practised (Map 1/40,000. 57D T. Square 14. 15. 20 + 21.	
	5	10.30AM	Manual training, all guns tested by firing one belt each. There are in excellent condition.	
		3 PM	Inspection of all Anti-Gas appliances by 10th Gas Officer	
	6		Very Heavy rains 32 new men from Routes given us to complete new establishment. 8 O.R. from each of 16. N.F. 16 L.F. 16 L.F. & 2 R. Innis. Fus.	
	7		Heavy rain all day. 1 OR arrived from base 2Lt S.B. JOHNSON + 2Lt G.E.R. COTTERILL arrived from M.G. Base.	
	8	10.30AM	Field scheme in a Pumpile	
	9	"	Company work all day. Sections attached to Routes for field scheme	
	10			
	11		Interior Economy & Company work.	
	12	10AM	Route March. 2Lt ELIAS to M.G. Base auth. G.O.C. 96 2nd Bde.	

WAR DIARY
or
INTELLIGENCE SUMMARY
(Erase heading not required.)

Army Form C. 2118

Page 2.

NOVEMBER 1916.

Place	Date	Hour	Summary of Events and Information	Remarks and references to Appendices
REREMPRE	Nov. 10	—	Company works all day.	
WARLOY	14	12 Noon	Marched from Rubillo to WARLOY	Ref. Map. Sheet 11 1/10,000 Lens
AVELUY	15.	3 am	Coy marched out to WARLOY to occupy dugouts in SOUTH BLUFF. Given truck in MARTINSART. Coy remained there in reserve for three days.	Ref. Map. 20,000 Trench Map
MAILLY MAILLET	17	9 AM	Coy marched from SOUTH BLUFF to Billets in MAILLY MAILLET	Ref Map. 57d S.E.
MAILLY MAILLET	18		Coy rested in billets at MAILLY-MAILLET. Section Officers reconnoitred Communication trenches to "WHITE CITY." "C" and "D" sections proceeded to dugouts at "WHITE CITY."	Ref Map. 20,000 Trench Map 57d S.E.
BEAUMONT HAMEL	19	7.30 p.m. 3 p.m. 6 p.m.	"C" and "D" sections relieved sections of 97th M.G. Coy at BEAUMONT-HAMEL. 2nd Lt. PARKER and 4 other ranks killed by shells, 6 other ranks wounded. "A" and "B" sections relieved 97th M.G. Coy at BEAUMONT HAMEL. 1 Wounded. COY. H.Q. at "WHITE CITY." Stores and Transport at MAILLY-MAILLET.	Ref. Map 20,000 Trench Map 57d S.E.
"	20		Coy in the line at BEAUMONT HAMEL. H.Q. at "WHITE CITY." Guns to fire only in case of counter-attack.	
"	21.	4 p.m.	Internal relief of sections — "A" and "B" exchanged positions with "C" and "D". 2/Lt ELIAS rejoined Coy from M.G. BASE.	
"	22		Coy remains in position. Forward gun positions heavily shelled during morning.	
"	23	3.30 p.m.	Raid on FRANKFURT TRENCH by 2nd INNISKILLINGS and 16th LANCS. One gun of "A" section fired indirect fire in support. Other guns prepared for counter-attack. 2/Lt. COLQUHOUN joined Coy.	

Army Form C. 2118

WAR DIARY
or
INTELLIGENCE SUMMARY
(Erase heading not required.)

Instructions regarding War Diaries and Intelligence Summaries are contained in F. S. Regs., Part II. and the Staff Manual respectively. Title Pages will be prepared in manuscript.

Place	Date	Hour	Summary of Events and Information	Remarks and references to Appendices
MAILLY MAILLET	24	10.30 a.m.	Cy relieved by 91st M.S.Coy. Marched to billets in MAILLY MAILLET. Ry map $\frac{1}{100,000}$ 2000 T. map. 57d S.E.	
AMPLIER	25	11.15 a.m	Cy travelled by motor buses to AMPLIER. Ry map. Sheet 11 $\frac{1}{100,000}$ LENS. 2/Lt. PARSONS and 1 O.R. to M.G. BASE, CAMIERS, for course of instruction.	
MONTRELET	26	9.30 a.m	Cy marched from AMPLIER to MONTRELET. Ry map. Sheet 11 $\frac{1}{100,000}$ LENS.	
MONTRELET	27		Cy work all day. — Physical Training; Gun cleaning and drives. Cleaning of Billets.	
"	28		C. O's Inspection of Cy. and Billets.	
"	29		Route March. 2/Lt. McCONNELL joined Cy.	
"	30		Ordinary Cy. work in forenoon. Football match in afternoon.	

J.J. Arthur Lt.
M.O. Cy.

96th Brigade.

32nd Division.

96th BRIGADE MACHINE GUN COMPANY

DECEMBER 1916

WAR DIARY
or
INTELLIGENCE SUMMARY

Army Form C. 2118

December 1916

Vol X

War Diary
96 M.G. Coy

Confidential

Original Copy

Army Form C. 2118

WAR DIARY
or
INTELLIGENCE SUMMARY
(Erase heading not required.)

Instructions regarding War Diaries and Intelligence Summaries are contained in F.S. Regs., Part II. and the Staff Manual respectively. Title Pages will be prepared in manuscript.

DECEMBER 1916.

Place	Date	Hour	Summary of Events and Information	Remarks and references to Appendices
MONTRELET	Dec. 1.	—	Marched to DOMART for Baths	H/m
	2.	11 AM	General inspection by acting G.O.C. 96 Bde	H/m
	3.	11 AM.	Church Parade	H/m
	4.		Company work. games during afternoon	H/m
	5.	9.30 AM	Inspection by G.O.C. 96 Inf Bde	H/m
	6.	10 AM	Inspection by G.O.C. V Corps.	H/m
	7.	9 AM	Route March - FIENVILLERS v. BERNVEIL. Ref Map LENS sheet 11.	H/m
	8.		Heavy rain. work on v-in Parallels	H/m
	9.		Firing on Range.	H/m
	10.	11 AM	Church Parade	H/m
	11.		Interior Coy work.	H/m
	12.		Interior Coy work + games	H/m
	13.	10.30 AM	Brigade Route March	H/m
	14.		Coy work. Gun drill + games.	H/m
	15.		General Interior economy. Coy on fatigue	H/m
	17.	11 AM.	Church Parade. 2/Lt. J.L.F. LEITCH joined from M.G. Team	H/m
	16.		Coy work in billets	H/m

Army Form C. 2118

WAR DIARY
or
INTELLIGENCE SUMMARY
(Erase heading not required.)

Instructions regarding War Diaries and Intelligence Summaries are contained in F.S. Regs., Part II. and the Staff Manual respectively. Title Pages will be prepared in manuscript.

Place	Date	Hour	Summary of Events and Information	Remarks and references to Appendices
MONTRELET	Dec 19	10AM	Simple Coy Tactical scheme.	
	20	"	Coy work & fatigues in billets	
	21st	"	Coy Route March. CANAPLES PERNOIS FIEFFES (new sheet 5" 1/100,000)	
	22	"	Action from twelve company work report	
	23	"	Elem Gun Training in billets	
	24	"	Church Parade 10 A.M.	
	25	"	Christmas day. Church Parade 10 A.M. The Coy had divine service altogether in the Recreation Room. At 2.30 P.M. the football match Section v final was played D. Section v. H.Q. V. The latter won by 3-1. A company concert was held in the Recreation Room at 6 P.M. It having obtained a piano & other being quite a fair amount of talent in the Company a very happy evening was spent.	
	26	10AM	Coy Route march. In the afternoon, a Gymkhana was held. In spite of wet day it was a great success	
	27	"	Range work M-G & Regular practice replaced by Bde Tactical Scheme.	
	28	"	Gun work in billets. Revetting practice.	
	29	"	Simple Tactical scheme in near? ground.	

Army Form C. 2118

WAR DIARY
or
INTELLIGENCE SUMMARY
(Erase heading not required.)

Instructions regarding War Diaries and Intelligence Summaries are contained in F. S. Regs., Part II. and the Staff Manual respectively. Title Pages will be prepared in manuscript.

Place	Date	Hour	Summary of Events and Information	Remarks and references to Appendices
MONTRELET	Dec 30	10 AM	Advanced gun drill.	
	31		Church Parade 10 A.M.	

Hamilton's Capt
Comdg 96th M.G. Coy

Army Form C. 2118

WAR DIARY
or
~~INTELLIGENCE SUMMARY~~

JANUARY *(Erase heading not required.)* 1917

Place	Date	Hour	Summary of Events and Information	Remarks and references to Appendices

WAR DIARY

96. MACHINE GUN. COY.

Volume X - JANUARY 1917

ORIGINAL COPY.

31/1/17

W. Williams Capt.
Commanding 96 M G Coy

WAR DIARY
or
INTELLIGENCE SUMMARY
(Erase heading not required.)

Army Form C. 2118

JANUARY 1917.

Place	Date	Hour	Summary of Events and Information	Remarks and references to Appendices
MONT RENET	JAN 1	10 AM	Coy on Fatigue	
"	2	"	Usual training + Coy work. One Officer and forward 15 Rfcc area we are about to move up to	
"	3	"	Brigade Route March & Tactical out put scheme	
"	4	"	Interior Economy work on Billets prior to moving out	
"	5	"	Coy prepared to vacate Billets	
"	6	9.30 AM	Coy marched out of billets to RAINCHEVAL. Ry Sheet 57 D 1/40,000. N. 12. C.	
RAINCHEVAL	7	10 AM	Marched from RAINCHEVAL to BUS (Div Rest area) Ry Sheet 67 D 1/40,000. J 26 central	
BUS	8	"	Taking over from 9th Coy Sudan. Officers went up to reconnoitre Yellow or defence line of sector	
"	9	"	Coy moved into Nissen Huts & prepared to go into the line to support an attack of 7th KOi.	
LINE HEBUTERNE SECTOR (South portion)	10	10.30 AM	The Coy received orders to support by Indirect Fire the attack of the 7th KOi on MUNICH TRENCH. For this purpose we were lent to XIII Corps & numbered in conjunction with the 92nd + 22nd M.G. Coys. The guns were emplaced in position by 4 PM on the ridge West of WATERLOO BRIDGE where a position was taken up at 20 yds interval from K 83.a.5.7 to 12 33.a.9.3. The positions were quite open being quite in the reverse slope. The Targets allotted were CHALK ABBEY & WHITE TRENCH. ranges from 2100 x & 2800 x with 50 x differences. Fire was at rate of 1 it 10 mm rapid 50 rds per mm for 10 mm + 25 rounds per min for 40 mins time to cease after 1 hr. Zero line was 6.40 AM. The operation was entirely successful & with MUNICH + MUCH TRENCHES the 7th KOi 10th about 100 prisoners. We remained in position until 4 PM 11/1/17 when coy re-ceded position & retained	Map Ref: HEBUTERNE 1/10,000 Trench map
	11	6.40 AM		

Army Form C. 2118

WAR DIARY
or
INTELLIGENCE SUMMARY
(Erase heading not required.)

JANUARY 1916

Place	Date	Hour	Summary of Events and Information	Remarks and references to Appendices
BUS	JAN 12	12	Coy returned to Pallets & prepared to take over from 97 M.G. Coy.	
"	13	10 AM	We relieved 97 Coy. C & D Sections carried out a rifle relief, in very difficult & muddy weather. C.Q.M.S. JOHNSON S. (No 1739) promoted No 15 + Coy. C.Q.M.S.	
"	14	10 AM	A + B sections marched to COURCELLES to relieve half 97 Coy who were in reserve the relay by whole Coy was effected without casualties.	
COURCELLES to HINX	15		Heavy snow accompanied by damp days, made trench work very dirty & uncomfortable & difficult. The trenches for the most part are in a bad condition & water-logged. The line is held by a system of out post & Lewis Gun strong points, while 4 or more M. Guns in what is ordinarily the support line (a T rench system. The main line of defence in the event of attack would be the Reserve (Village Line) line - or Yellow line. Most of the gun positions have good dugouts but an almost inaccessible by day without undue risk for exposure or betraying locality of position.	
"	16		Coy H'Q'rs times came in COURCELLES. it was decided that it would work better if the section do the whole of the Brigade Tour & so the remaining section in reserve carried rations rifle to the gun position dugouts. The weather turned very cold & severe frosts are being experienced	
"	17		the weather has become still colder & a good deal of snow has fallen. The trenches are now for the most part hard & dry by frost but very slippery. Lieut R de ICE. Lt DAWSON (from 69 M.G.C.) has become 2nd in command	

WAR DIARY or INTELLIGENCE SUMMARY

Army Form C. 2118

JANUARY 1917

Place	Date	Hour	Summary of Events and Information	Remarks and references to Appendices
In the LINE	JAN 17		Arrangements were made to hand over the left Batt Sub Sector to 35 Inf Bde. 19.10 w. to take over the whole of 7th 10 in sector. 2Lr. DONNER reported for duty (from M.G.Base.)	(Kh)
	18 + 19		On the night of 18/19 Jan 6 5"M.G.C. took over 6 guns from us becoming in with 2 in the line. The guns given up were situated generally along BRISOUX-CABER TRENCH line between JENA & NAIRN TRENCHES. The relief was carried out cautiously without casualties. The condition of the trenches however caused much delay in arranging gun kit. LT. GARDINER from M.G.Base.	(KW)
	19 + 20		We took over 6 guns from 14 M. G.C. who were going out from 15 infantry over entire portion of Divisional Sector. Most of the positions are difficult to locate & can only be visited with any security by night. A+B Sections are in line	(W)
COURCELLES	21.	2 P.M.	Coy Hd Qrs are now moved to MAILLY-MAILLET the Coy less A+B Sections & two gun teams of C Section marched to new to billeting area.	(W)
"	22 + 23		We & surgave up our 3 right flank guns to 14 M. G.C. who came in again on our right. This left us with 7 guns in the line so we moved the number up to 8. for the Brigade trench area which has now become held on left Brigade of the to waren holding from NAIRN to DELAUNAY (inclusive) 3 5" M. G.C. (19 10 in.) are on our left & 14 M. G.C. (32 10 in) on our right. We is now hew all these Brigades in the line. The Brigade lst Line Transport moved from BUS lo BERTRANCOURT	(KW)

Army Form C. 2118

WAR DIARY
or
INTELLIGENCE SUMMARY
(Erase heading not required.)

JANUARY 1917

Place	Date	Hour	Summary of Events and Information	Remarks and references to Appendices
In line	JAN 23		Q. Martin stores in the village & Transport lines at T. 27 d. 2.2. Ref 57D to 40,000 (Sucres & Trailers were taken over from 2/2 M. G.C. 7th Novw).	
	24		Indirect fire is carried out nightly on roads & tracks detailed by Bde H.Q. The rations and rum to the gun teams by the mlms in reserve, still coming up as far as EUSTON DUMP. Internal reliefs have been every 8 days.	
	25.	6.20 AM	The enemy artillery had been very active during the night + at "stand to" he got a direct "which" bag "hit on a dugout entrance causing casualties of 2 O.R. killed (1 Sergt) 3 O.R. wounded. (1 a corporal).	
	26. 27		Indirect fire at the rate of about 1000 rds per night. Enemy cattle reply from enemy M. Guns. The weather is extremely cold & trench conditions most trying. In spite of this the casualties in the Coy. is very little.	
	28		The section on whole quiet. One casualty from shrapnel.	
	29	3PM	Internal relief of C+D sections by A+B. No casualties.	
	30 31		Line very quiet. More snow falling. The roads are very dangerous especially in direct from were carried out in conjunction with Artillery on K. 36. b. 3 16 K. 36 b. 7 g	

Maps Refs. Trench HEBUTERNE 57D NE 3+4 (parts of)/10,000
Area Map 57D 1/40,000

Weather 1st week cold wet & unhealthy
Remainder Very cold. Snow & frosty.

J.A. Williams Capt
Comdg 96 M.G.C.

1875 Wt. W593/826 1,000,000 4/15 J.B.C. & A. A.D.S.S./Forms/C. 2118.

WAR DIARY or INTELLIGENCE SUMMARY

Army Form C. 2118

FEBRUARY 1917

Vol 12

War Diary Vol. XII

96 Machine Gun Coy.

Original

7 to 28th 1917.

H. Williams Capt.
Commanding 96 M.G.C.

Army Form C. 2118

WAR DIARY
or
INTELLIGENCE SUMMARY
(Erase heading not required.)

FEBRUARY 1917

Place	Date	Hour	Summary of Events and Information	Remarks and references to Appendices
LINE (out) BEAUMONT	Feb. 1		Sector very quiet with much less Artillery activity than usual.	
HAMEL-SERRE Sector	2		Coy Relieved by 5th M.G.C. (9/190w) - to begin a wide stepping towards BEAUMONT. HAMEL. 5th Coy only took over to relieve guns pending relief without casualties	
	3		Coy in Billets in MAILLY MAILLET.	
	4		6 guns lent 16 97 Coy for use before BEAUMONT-HAMEL. 97 Coy have control of 26 Vickers guns in a Brigade front which occupy forward posts. Three 6 guns are disposed of, 4 in line & 2 in reserve at MAILLY. 1 casualty wounded	
	5		The 2 guns in MAILLY sent forward to line 2 killed & 2 wounded by our own artillery (62 w 16 pdrs regulating	
	6 Night Dusk		Two 6 guns into forward posts 1 relieve 97 Coy guns. These guns are D Section & 27 J C Section. Weather is much warmer & these carried trenches & very muddy	
	8		3 casualties in posts - two killed - no wounded. Posts can only be reached by night	
	9 N/M 16	6.30 PM	97 Bde made a successful attack taking over 200 prisoners.	
	11		D sect. relieved by B & 2 guns J C relieved by rest J C.	
	12	10 mls	Our guns again occupy posts 6 many counterattacks on our left.	
	13	"	Much heavy artillery & German Counter attack	
	14		96 Inf Bde move out & we are attached to 62 Div. in 10 w Reserve until 15 Inf Bde	
	15		Line quiet - weather much warmer.	

Army Form C. 2118

WAR DIARY
or
INTELLIGENCE SUMMARY
(Erase heading not required.)

FEBRUARY 1917

Instructions regarding War Diaries and Intelligence Summaries are contained in F. S. Regs., Part II. and the Staff Manual respectively. Title Pages will be prepared in manuscript.

Place	Date	Hour	Summary of Events and Information	Remarks and references to Appendices
LINE	FEB 16	7 PM	Order from I Corps to place 2 guns at ammunition dumps at each of T.20.C.1.4. T.9.d.9.9. T.13.d.2.2. Ref. 40.000 57.D. There are 10 guns agst aeroplanes raid. A section placed B in Pate under 97 Coy.	
	17 Night 18	Dusk	Our 6 guns should be relieved by 91 Coy of 7 Div. who arrived very late & the relief orders were muddled up. Consequently 97 Coy men only got to bivouac of our lorries but. The remaining three had to stay until 9/19.	
HARPONVILLE	18	2.30 PM	Coy marched to HARPONVILLE (U.S.C central 40.000 57.D.) Village under martial law because of numerous fires. One gun team of A section managed to assume at the village at 3 AM.	
FLESSELLES	19	10.30 AM	Coy marched to FLESSELLES. Heard Mr COLQUHOUN & the 2 remaining guns leaving A reported on by motor lorry from the line at MAILLY-MAILLET, IRFRIERWATER & FRNL from M. G. Base.	
AMIENS	20	11 AM	Coy marched to billets at ST ACHEUL (AMIENS)	
THENNES	21	10 AM	Coy marched to THENNES.	
"	22		Coy refitted & drew clothes. Mr G.D HAMILTON joined from M.G. Base.	
BEAUCOURT	23	10.15 AM	Coy marched into a Div area under IV Corps preparatory to taking over from the FRENCH. The billets were good much pitted up but the roads in places were almost impassable.	
NARVILLERS	24	1.30 PM	Section officers reconnoitred the line at the Coy moved into dugouts at WARVILLERS. Ref. 66.c NE & 66.d NW (Tranks)	

Army Form C. 2118

WAR DIARY
or
INTELLIGENCE SUMMARY
(Erase heading not required.)

FEBRUARY 1917

Place	Date	Hour	Summary of Events and Information	Remarks and references to Appendices
WARVILLERS	Feb 25th Night 26.	Dusk	Coy takes over from FRENCH at dusk. — 16 guns in the line — 10 in support positions and 6 in reserve ones. Weather windy and extra quiet. Altering emplacements to suit mark III K/gd	
	2) 28		Weather calm and mild. Building and altering emplacements	

H. Williams Capt.
Comd'g 96 M.G. Coy

Vol 13

W A R   D I A R Y.

of

96th Machine Gun Company.

MARCH 1917.

Vol. 13.

WAR DIARY

Vol. 13

96 Machine Gun Coy

March 1917.

Original Copy

[signature] Capt.
Commdg 96 M.C—e
31/3/17.

WAR DIARY or INTELLIGENCE SUMMARY

Army Form C. 2118.

MARCH 1917

Place	Date	Hour	Summary of Events and Information	Remarks and references to Appendices
MARCH LINE	1	—	The Sector continued to be quiet. Intermittent fire was kept up to the extent of 6000 rpr per day.	
	2	—	Enemy actively engaged principally of GATCHILLE and ROUVROY & WARVILLERS during the evening	
	3 night	Dusk	We were relieved by 97 Coy & returned to billets in BEAUCOURT. Relief different owing to extended front	
BEAUCOURT	4 5		& took 8 hrs to accomplish. It was completed by 4 AM Carnoilles N.I.	
"	6 7 8		Coy in rest completing stores & overhauling guns. The guns during this period were examined by 1st Div. Ammunition Staff & pronounced fit & in good condition.	
"	9 10	night		
LINE	11	Dusk	Relieved 114 M.G. Coy in right sub sector. N° Casualties. Map Ref 66 NE & 66B NW fourth [of] Trench 20,000	
"	12		Line generally quiet with fine about 1000 rds per day	
"	13	night	Preparations made to assist FRENCH attack on our right during day time	
"	14	night	but also our own portion & fire still maintained at the av[erage] 1000 & 10000 per day	
"	15	10 PM	2nd Lt. J. R. COLQUHOUN wounded in leg by an M.G. bullet	
"	16-17	7 AM	Together well above from 97 Coy Barrage fire was maintained from 7-9 AM aimed on R.3.a.2 & 16 R.10.c.5.5. lifting at 8 AM to R.3.c.5.5 & R.4.c.9.5 & firing till 9.15 AM. The 20 guns engaged used 110,000 rds. The FORMEN Barrage was from the sky & unable to its ROYE - S. ANNENNES met with little opposition. The enemy had vacated his line. Ref. Trench Map 62 S.E. 20,000.	See APPENDIX I
"	17/18	Night	Our guns went forward & occupied an old line trenches. The Bn. went forward in pursuit of enemy Coy occupied Cattle ruins & marched to CREMERY by way of FARVILLERS (Ref AMIENS N.W. 40000)	
CREMERY	18	2 PM		
NESLE & BACQUENCOURT	19	2 PM	Marched to NESLE & prepared to occupy an outpost line along the SOMME Run from OFFOY-BURY. Ist Butt in front two held in support & late in Reserve at BACQUENCOURT. One 1/2 section was attached to each Butt & the remaining 8 guns in reserve. The line was taken up & fully occupied by 7 PM m30 incl. The nearest guns were in BACQUENCOURT by 4 PM 19th. Map Ref 62D — Coy H.Q. were at I.34.d.5.e.	

A8834 Wt. W4973/M687 750,000 8/16 D.D. & L. Ltd. Forms/C.2118/13.

WAR DIARY
or
INTELLIGENCE SUMMARY.
(Erase heading not required.)

Army Form C. 2118.

Instructions regarding War Diaries and Intelligence Summaries are contained in F. S. Regs., Part II. and the Staff Manual respectively. Title pages will be prepared in manuscript.

Place	Date	Hour	Summary of Events and Information	Remarks and references to Appendices
BACQUENCOURT – OFFOY	MAR 20	-	96 Bde occupied an out post line TRULE-MATIGNY with orders to defend GOMME bridges. Two sections were detailed to defend the villages & one section the approaches to the river at OFFOY. The remainder were in reserve at Coy H.Qr. ref map Sheet 66D 4 inch T.	
	21	-	Coy employed digging gun emplacements for the Bridgehead defences of the SOMME at OFFOY	
	22	-	Coy in reserve employed ating emplacements in the main line of defence West of SOMME	
	23	-	Bridges were prepared for withdrawal of forward guns by way of details through the marshy wood to OFFOY.	
	24	-	Emplacements were completed & shelters undertaken.	
	25	-	Alternate emplacements were constructed & the bridges generally improved	
	26	-	Coy in reserve refitted with clothing	
	27	-		
	28	-	On fatigue in Reserve Coy in line & outposts relieving 4/4th	
TOUEE	29	9AM.	Coy Move to TOUEE in Div Reserve. 97 + 14 Brigade go through us to establish new forward line Cleaning billets from debris & repairing of timbers.	
	30	-		
GERMAINE	31	12Noon	Coy moved up to support 97 Bde in an attack	
			Weather Fairly Normal. Rain & snow intermittent	

H.R. Williams Capt
O.C. 96 M.G. Coy

Vol XIII WAR DIARY APPENDIX I

96 M G Coy Operation Order No 15.

1. In accordance with offensive operations mentioned to you

2. You will lay your guns so as to be able to put up a barrage
   A R 3 a 5 3 — R 10 b 5.5
   B L 33 d 0.2   R 4 b 9.5

3. You will fire on A Lines as follows
   Zero – Zero + 60 min   rapid fire 100 rnds a min
   Zero + 60 – Zero + 120   50 rnds per min

4. You will arrange to fire on B lines as follows
   Zero + 120 min – Zero + 3½ hrs   25 rnds per min
   After which time you will remain on B Lines & will fire as the situation demands or on an S.O.S call

5. Great care must be taken to ensure absolute accuracy in setting your guns, & the time laid down for changing from A to B lines must be strictly adhered to.

6. Very close liaison will be kept with Batt'n Commanders.

7. My Hd Q's will be at L 31 A 8.4, to which place reports should be sent when the situation has cleared.

8. Zero is at 7 A.M March 17th
9. Stores will remain at LA RAPERIE
10. Acknowledge

J A Williams Cpt
Cmd'g 96 M G Coy.

CONFIDENTIAL.

Vol/14

WAR DIARY.

OF

96th MACHINE GUN COMPANY.

From 1st April 1917.

To 30th April 1917.

Army Form C. 2118.

WAR DIARY
or
INTELLIGENCE SUMMARY.
(Erase heading not required.)

APRIL 1917.

Instructions regarding War Diaries and Intelligence Summaries are contained in F. S. Regs., Part II and the Staff Manual respectively. Title pages will be prepared in manuscript.

Place	Date	Hour	Summary of Events and Information	Remarks and references to Appendices
LINE. H.Qrs at GERMAINE	APRIL Night 1	11 P.M.	Coy moved up from SANCOURT to GERMAINE, arriving at 2 P.M. At 11 P.M. Coy moved up to support an attack of 97 Bde on SAVY. 16 guns were placed at X.26.C. in a sunken road as barrage set up along southern edge of BOIS D'HOLNON. The attack was timed for 5 A.M. The 97 Bde suffered few casualties & were completely successful. We had no casualties & guns were withdrawn at 7 A.M. to GERMAINE.	Ref. Map ST QUENTIN 1/100,000 N.W.R. Ref Sheet 62 c 1/40,000
SAVY WOOD	2	10 A.M.	Orders were received to march to rôle at Attency in valley S.W. of VAUX. The Bde was to attack SAVY WOOD at 3 P.M. 4 guns were attached to each Batt. The attack was successful & the Bde pushed on to take Pt. 132. (3.15.d.7.0.) We fairly heavy casualties resulted but their high ground commanding ST QUENTIN was finally taken together with 2 heavy 77 mm batting & a Machine Gun. We suffered one casualty (killed).	Ref Sheet 62 B 1/40,000
	3		The Bde front in advance of BOIS de SAVY was consolidated & suffered much enemy shelling. The weather was unsettled to a degree. Very heavy rains & finally snow had what shelling they used in prevail. There were only three aero of our guns out of action & the men confirmed to be excellent.	M/K
	4	3 P.M.	From quarry by Pt. 136 we supported with barrage fire by 12 guns a successful & FRENCH attack on DALLON. During the evening a shell fell on our gun out of action. For excellent work during the operations the following were recommended for honours. No. 7870. Sergt. NEAL. W.G. No. 6790. Pte. McFALL A. No. 8462. Pte. LEPPINGTON R. } Military Medals.	M/K

Army Form C. 2118.

WAR DIARY
or
INTELLIGENCE SUMMARY.
(Erase heading not required.)

Instructions regarding War Diaries and Intelligence Summaries are contained in F.S. Regs., Part II. and the Staff Manual respectively. Title pages will be prepared in manuscript.

Place	Date	Hour	Summary of Events and Information	Remarks and references to Appendices
SAVY	APRIL 5		The weather was very bad, much snow + sleet. The enemy shelling was very heavy around SAVY wood.	M/S
"	6		Weather much improved & less shelling. Complete enemy M.G. was silenced + sent to Div H.Q.	M/S
"	7	8 PM	We was on our left. 61st + 5th made a successful attack. Retook the line + important north side of St QUENTIN FRESNOY-LE-PETIT + GRICOURT were occupied.	M/S
"	8		Enemy shelling on our front was heavy. We had one casualty & a few knocked out by shrapnel. Lt DAWSON assumed Temp Comd of BIG M.G. Coy	M/S
"	9		Very high winds + rain with a heavy fall of snow in the afternoon	M/S
"	10		Weather slightly improved, but winds still high. Pt. 138 heavily shelled in the afternoon. No casualties.	M/S
FORESTE	11			M/S
"	12	11 a.m.	Company relieved by W.I. M.G. Coy, sections marched independently to billets in FORESTE Lt SIMPSON proceeded to 106th M.G. Coy as Second in Command	M/S
"	13		Company in rest at FORESTE, under 1 hours notice. At 7.30 p.m. men had baths at GERMAINE	M/S
LINE FRANCILLY H.Q.	14	9 a.m.	Company marched to ATILLY, Attached to 97th Bde. At 6 p.m. 4 sections proceeded into line and took up positions in front of FAYET, under O.C. 97th M.G. Coy. H.Q. at FRANCILLY. Their are now 48 to guns on 97th Bde frontage	M/S
LINE H.Q. ATILLY	15		97th Bde relieved by 96th. Company/guns extended over Bde front to cover ground formerly swept by 48 machine guns. FAYET heavily shelled from St QUENTIN direction and East of GRICOURT. Coy H.Q. moved to ATILLY. Several casualties during the day by shell fire. Weather fine.	M/S
"	16		In line in front of FAYET. Village again heavily shelled, causing many infantry casualties. Lt DAWSON rejoined company. 2/Lt GRIFFITHS joined the Company	M/S
"	17	3 p.m.	8 guns moved back to occupy reserve positions on FRESNOY-SELENCY-FRANCILLY line of resistance. Other 8 guns remain in position defending FAYET. Weather cloudy and windy, with snow at night.	M/S

A.5834 Wt. W4973/M687 750,000 8/16 D. D. & L. Ltd. Forms/C.2118/13.

Army Form C. 2118.

WAR DIARY
or
INTELLIGENCE SUMMARY.
(Erase heading not required.)

Instructions regarding War Diaries and Intelligence Summaries are contained in F.S. Regs. Part II. and the Staff Manual respectively. Title pages will be prepared in manuscript.

Place	Date	Hour	Summary of Events and Information	Remarks and references to Appendices
LINE HQ ATILLY	APRIL 18		Company remain in position. Heavy some artillery causing much discomfort, as men have merely improved shelters. Continued shelling of FAYET, and FAYET-FRESNOY road.	N/A
"	19		Company remain in position. Weather slightly improved, but still dull. 16 gun emplacements made in FRESNOY-SELENCY-FRAMILLY line of resistance. Fatigue party of R.E.s commenced dug-outs for gun teams.	N/A
ATILLY FORESTE	20	4.30 p.m.	Company relieved by 184th M.G. Coy. (61st Divison). Relief proceeded independently to billets at FORESTE. The day was quiet on the front, and the weather much improved.	N/A
FORESTE ATHIES	21	2 p.m.	Company marched from FORESTE to billets in ATHIES. Weather continued fine.	N/A
ATHIES	22		Company in rest. Men spent the day in bathing and cleaning equipment. Weather excellent.	N/A
"	23	2 p.m.	At ATHIES. Foreman – Physical drill; Limber cleaning; cleaning and arranging gun stores. Inspection by Commanding Officer at 2 p.m. Weather continues excellent.	N/A
"	24		At ATHIES. Forenoon – Gas Physical drill; Gun drill and Musketeon. Gun cleaning. Afternoon – Football.	N/A
"	25		At ATHIES. Forenoon – Physical drill; Guns tested on improvised range to N.E. of ATHIES. All in good condition. Gun cleaning. Afternoon – Football. Weather still excellent.	N/A
"	26		At ATHIES. Instruction was given in firing practice on range in forenoon. Sun cleaning. Afternoon – Football.	N/A
"	27		At ATHIES. Forenoon – Running; physical drill; gun drill. Inspection of gas appliances by Divisional gas N.C.O. Weather still dry and fine. Afternoon – Football.	N/A

Army Form C. 2118.

WAR DIARY
or
INTELLIGENCE SUMMARY.
(Erase heading not required.)

Instructions regarding War Diaries and Intelligence Summaries are contained in F. S. Regs., Part II. and the Staff Manual respectively. Title pages will be prepared in manuscript.

Place	Date	Hour	Summary of Events and Information	Remarks and references to Appendices
ATHIES.	28.		In hut at ATHIES. Forenoon - Running and physical drill; baths; instruction in German M. gun; Lewis gun drill and cleaning. Afternoon - Football.	WF
"	29.		Church parade in morning. Recognising game for demonstration of Indirect Fire to Brigade in afternoon.	h/p
"	30.		At ATHIES. Gun drill and Lewis Cleaning. Indirect Fire looked on ground chosen to TEST g ATHIES. Afternoon, Company baths. Weather still excellent.	WF

W.J.Anson Lieut
O.C. 96 M.G. Company

A.5834 Wt W.4973/M687 750,000 8/16 D. D. & L. Ltd. Forms/C.2118/13.

Army Form C. 2118.

WAR DIARY
or
INTELLIGENCE SUMMARY.
(Erase heading not required.)

Vol 5

WAR DIARY of
96 Machine Gun Company

May 1st 1917 to May 31st 1917

Vol XIV

H Williams Capt
O.C. 96 M.G.Coy

WAR DIARY or INTELLIGENCE SUMMARY.

(Erase heading not required.)

Army Form C. 2118

Instructions regarding War Diaries and Intelligence Summaries are contained in F. S. Regs., Part II. and the Staff Manual respectively. Title pages will be prepared in manuscript.

Map... 62...

Place	Date	Hour	Summary of Events and Information	Remarks and references to Appendices
ATHIES	May 1917 1	10 a.m.	Inspection of Brigade by new General. Weather tropical. Afternoon — Football and bathing. Lt DAWSON in temp. command of Company.	11A/1
"	2		Forenoon — Gun drill. Cleaning of guns, equipment, and clothing. Afternoon — C.O's. Inspection at 2 p.m. Thereafter — re-section.	11A/
"	3	10 a.m.	Inspection of Brigade by Corps General. Brigade complimented on its recent work. Weather still very warm. Afternoon — Football, inter-section.	11A/
"	4		Forenoon — Practice for an approaching demonstration of Indirect Fire to Brigade, on ground East of ST. CHRIST. Inspection of all Gas appliances.	11A/
"	5		Forenoon — Physical drill. Elementary and advanced Gun Drill. Practice for demonstration continued with two guns. Firing during the night. Afternoon — Football. 31 rounds very accurate.	11A/
"	6	2.30 p.m.	Church Parade in the forenoon. At 2.30 p.m. demonstration of Indirect Fire to Brigade. 48,000 rounds were fired. had rain outright. accurate. observation very difficult.	11A/
"	7		Forenoon — Physical drill. Belt-filling and Gun and Spare Parts Cleaning. Afternoon — Continuation of Belt-filling. Heavy Rain all night.	11A/

WAR DIARY
or
INTELLIGENCE SUMMARY.
(Erase heading not required.)

Army Form C. 2118.

Instructions regarding War Diaries and Intelligence Summaries are contained in F. S. Regs., Part II. and the Staff Manual respectively. Title pages will be prepared in manuscript.

Place	Date	Hour	Summary of Events and Information	Remarks and references to Appendices
ATHIES	May 8		Heavy rain all afternoon. Parade Cancelled. Several of our billets were flooded out. No outdoor work possible, as rain kept on intermittently all day.	
"	9		Sections attached to Infantry Battalions for tactical schemes. Weather again fine. Football in afternoon.	
"	10		Physical Drill. Gun drill. Section Instruction class in Elementary Gun drill. Special instruction in use of German Machine Gun. C.O. Rehearsed men leave to U.K. Slight rain in the evening. Football in afternoon, and bathing.	
"	11		Physical Drill. Instruction class in Elementary Gun drill. Practice on miniature Range between ATHIES and ENNEMAIN. Afternoon — Gun cleaning and Ball-Filling.	
"	12		Forenoon — Physical Drill. Tactical Schemes by sections by sections under Lectures Officers, Scheme to include particularly 'Action from Limbers'. Afternoon — Football, and practice for Company Sports.	
"	13		Forenoon — Church Parade. Afternoon and Evening — Company Sports, and Football Tournament.	
"	14	9a.m.	Forenoon — Brigade Tactical Scheme. Capture of ST. CHRIST. Three sections put up Barrage; One section advanced with 8 attacking infantry. Afternoon — Football.	
"	15		Forenoon — One section with 15th LANCS. repeated yesterdays Bde. Scheme. Other section — Physical drill, Gun drill. Afternoon — Cleaning and Packing Limbers. Recreation.	

Army Form C. 2118.

WAR DIARY
or
INTELLIGENCE SUMMARY.
(Erase heading not required.)

Instructions regarding War Diaries and Intelligence Summaries are contained in F. S. Regs., Part II. and the Staff Manual respectively. Title pages will be prepared in manuscript.

Place	Date May	Hour	Summary of Events and Information	Remarks and references to Appendices
ATHIES — LICOURT	16	5 a.m.	Parade 5.a.m. Company marched from ATHIES to LICOURT, reaching billets about 8.a.m. Rested at LICOURT for remainder of day.	47.
LICOURT — ROSIÈRES	17	4.45 a.m.	Parade 4.45 a.m. Company marched from LICOURT to ROSIÈRES, reaching billets about 10 a.m. Rested at ROSIÈRES.	112.
ROSIÈRES	18		In billets at ROSIÈRES. Cleaning Guns, Gun Stores, and Limbers, in Johnson. Afternoon — Recreation.	111.
"	19		Forenoon — Physical Drill ; Elementary and Advanced Gun Drill. Gun Cleaning. Afternoon — Recreation.	30/5/1
"	20		Forenoon — Church Parade. 2/Lt. S.F.R. COTTERILL & Company to return to GRANTHAM. 2/Lt. W.S. ELIAS on leave to U.K. 2/Lt. G.D. HAMILTON returned to Company from course at M.G. BASE SCHOOL 2/Lt. C.S. GRUNDY joined Company.	41.
"	21		Forenoon — Physical Drill. Tactical Work under Section Officers. Company inoculated to-day. Men rested in billets.	114.
"	22			115.
"	23	10 a.m.	Brigade Tactical Scheme near MEHARICOURT. Company carried out usual tactics of 3 Section — Barrage Fire 1 Section in Advance with Infantry to Consolidate.	116.
"	24		Forenoon — Physical Drill. Elementary and Advanced Gun Drill. Stores. Afternoon — Recreation.	117.

WAR DIARY
or
INTELLIGENCE SUMMARY.
(Erase heading not required.)

Army Form C. 2118.

Place	Date May	Hour	Summary of Events and Information	Remarks and references to Appendices
ROSIÈRES	25		Recreation and Sports Training, by Bde. permission; Joanon and afternoon.	
"	26		Forenoon — Physical Drill. Bath. Afternoon — Bde. Sports on Ground between ROSIÈRES and CAIX. Company won 8 prizes.	
"	27		Forenoon — Church Parade. Lt. DAWSON on 3 days leave to PARIS. Afternoon — Recreation. Officers were inoculated today.	
"	28		Forenoon — Physical Drill. Firing Gun on Miniature Range. Gun Cleaning. Afternoon — Recreation. Belt Filling.	
"	29		Forenoon — Physical Drill. Gun and Limber Cleaning. Afternoon — Limber packing.	
ROSIÈRES — WIENCOURT	30	9.32 a.m.	Company marched from ROSIÈRES to WIENCOURT, reaching billets about 10.15 a.m. Rested during remainder of day.	
WIENCOURT	31		In rest at WIENCOURT. Inspection Parade under Section Officers.	

H.M. Williams. Capt.
O.C. 96? M.G. Coy

Army Form C. 2118.

WAR DIARY
or
INTELLIGENCE SUMMARY.
(Erase heading not required.)

Vol 16

WAR DIARY
OF
96th M.G. Company
VOL 15
1/6/17 — 30/6/17

1/7/17

J.H. Williams Capt
O.C. 96 M.G. Coy

WAR DIARY
or
INTELLIGENCE SUMMARY.

(Erase heading not required.)

Army Form C. 2118.

Instructions regarding War Diaries and Intelligence Summaries are contained in F. S. Regs., Part II. and the Staff Manual respectively. Title pages will be prepared in manuscript.

Place	Date	Hour	Summary of Events and Information	Remarks and references to Appendices
GILLAUCOURT —CAESTRE —LA COURONNE	June 1918 1	3 a.m.	Coy. Qr. GILLAUCOURT by train at 3 a.m. via ABBEVILLE, ETAPLES, BOULOGNE, CALAIS, ST. OMER, HAZEBROUCK to CAESTRE. Detrained at 4 p.m. and marched to billets at LA COURONNE. Ref: map 1/100,000 HAZEBROUCK 5A. Transport picked up in the open.	HW
LA COURONNE	2		Forenoon — Cleaning and Readjustment of kimbers. All Guns, Spare Parts and Gun Stores checked and cleaned. Afternoon — Inspection under Section Officers' arrangement.	HW
"	3		Forenoon — Physical Drill 8.30 a.m. Church Parades. The Commanding Officer reconnoitred the approaches to WULVERGHEM and PLOEGSTEERT. Afternoon — Lt. W. S. ELIAS rejoined Coy. from leave to U.K.	HW
"	4	8 a.m.	Battre turn-out in battle order in half an hour, under Brigade supervision. Coy. reached starting point, first, in 21 minutes. Thereafter a short route march via BLEU and VIEUX BERQUIN. Head to offences. Coy. rested in billets all afternoon.	HW
"	5		Forenoon — Section Officers reconnoitred the approaches to WULVERGHEM and PLOEGSTEERT, and studied model of German trenches around MESSINES. Coy. did Physical Drill and Gun Drill in vicinity of billets. This is very little training ground here. Dance in the evening.	HW

Army Form C. 2118.

WAR DIARY
or
INTELLIGENCE SUMMARY
(Erase heading not required.)

Instructions regarding War Diaries and Intelligence Summaries are contained in F. S. Regs., Part II. and the Staff Manual respectively. Title pages will be prepared in manuscript.

Place	Date June 1917	Hour	Summary of Events and Information	Remarks and references to Appendices
LA COURONNE	6	9 a.m.	6.30 a.m. Games. 8 a.m. Physical Drill. 9 a.m. Short route march combined with practice in "Action from Limbers". Location — Road and fields to S.W. of BLEU. 37nd Division is attached to II ANZAC Corps, which is to attack MESSINES. Our Coy. is confined to billets from this evening & to be ready to move up if required.	WW
"	7.		"Zero day" for II ANZAC Corps. Coy. still confined to billets. 6.30 a.m. Games. 8 a.m. Physical Drill. 9 — 12.30. Gun drill, mechanism and stoppages in billets under Section Officers. The attack on MESSINES is reported a great success.	WW
"	8		Coy. still confined to billets. Games. Physical Drill. Gun drill etc. carried out as yesterday. II ANZACS entirely successful. Orders to remain in billets cancelled late this evening.	WW
"	9	9 a.m.	Forenoon — 6.30 a.m. Games. 8 a.m. Physical Drill. 9 a.m. Tactical Exercise including "Action from Limbers" and Concealment of Gun Positions, in vicinity of BLEU.	WW
		2.30 pm	Parade for Limber cleaning and packing. Games in the evening. LT. D GARDNER to M.G. SCHOOL CAMIERS.	
"	10.		Church Parade R.C. 9 a.m. at VIEUX BERQUIN. C of E 11 a.m. " " Wes. 11 a.m. near BLEU. The Parades in the afternoon	WW

A8834 Wt. W4973/M687 750,000 8.16 D. D. & L. Ltd. Forms/C.2118/13

Army Form C. 2118.

WAR DIARY
or
INTELLIGENCE SUMMARY.
(Erase heading not required.)

Instructions regarding War Diaries and Intelligence Summaries are contained in F. S. Regs., Part II. and the Staff Manual respectively. Title pages will be prepared in manuscript.

Place	Date	Hour	Summary of Events and Information	Remarks and references to Appendices
LA COURONNE	June 1917 11.		Forenoon — all Box Respirators fitted with new attachment, an improved inlet valve, and additional chemical. Inspection of all equipment and kit by Section Officers. Afternoon — All Lewis Stores etc. packed in limbers in preparation for move tomorrow.	MW
LA COURONNE —LE CARREAU	12	8.30 a.m.	Coy. marched from LA COURONNE to billets in LE CARREAU. (Ref. Map HAZEBROUCK 5-A 1/100,000). Heat was very great, but no men fell out. Reached LE CARREAU 12 noon. Coy. rested in afternoon. 2/Lt. J. B. NEILSON on leave to U.K.	MW
LE CARREAU —WORM-HOUDT.	13	8.30 a.m.	Coy. marched from LE CARREAU to tents at Eq. WORMHOUDT. Rested at WORMHOUDT. Ref. Map HAZEBROUCK 5-A 1/100,000. Lt. DAWSON went on in advance to reconnoitre line in front of NIEUPORT.	MW
WORMHOUDT.	14		Coy. in rest at WORMHOUDT. Lewis gun and limber cleaning only.	MW
WORMHOUDT —UXEM.	15	9.15 a.m.	Coy. marched from WORMHOUDT to UXEM, a distance of 18 Kilos, via BERGUES. Complimented by General. (Ref. Map Dunkerque 1A 1/100,000). Afternoon — bathing in the canal close to billets.	MW

WAR DIARY
or
INTELLIGENCE SUMMARY.

Army Form C. 2118.

(Erase heading not required.)

Place	Date	Hour	Summary of Events and Information	Remarks and references to Appendices
UXEM	June 16/17		Coy in rest at UXEM. Inspection under Section Officers arrangement. Advanced Gun Drill and Gun Cleaning. Bathing in Canal close to billets. afternoon.	MW
"	17.		Coy in rest at UXEM. Games; Physical Drill; Mechanism and 'I.A.' Limber Cleaning and packing. Bathing afternoon.	MW
UXEM - LEFFRINCKHOUCKE - COXYDE.	18.		Coy marched from UXEM to railway beyond LEFFRINCKHOUCKE. Thence by rail via ADINKERKE. Detrained near COXYDE, and marched to billets in hut in CAMP "JEAN BARK", to E of COXYDE. Transport came by road from UXEM, via GHYVELDE, ADENKERKE, FURNES, COXYDE. Ref. Map. DUNKERQUE 1A 1/100,000.	MW
COXYDE (CAMP "JEAN BARK")	19.		Coy in rest at CAMP "JEAN BARK". General "Cleaning up". Checking of Gun Stores ek. Advanced gun drill among sand-dunes behind Camp. No parades in the afternoon.	M
	20.		Coy in rest. Physical Drill. Inspection under Section Officers. Visual Training and Judging distance. No afternoon parades.	M

WAR DIARY
or
INTELLIGENCE SUMMARY

(Erase heading not required.)

Army Form C. 2118.

Instructions regarding War Diaries and Intelligence Summaries are contained in F.S. Regs., Part II. and the Staff Manual respectively. Title pages will be prepared in manuscript.

Place	Date	Hour	Summary of Events and Information	Remarks and references to Appendices
COXYDE (Camp JEAN BART:)	June 1917 21.	9 a.m. 2.30pm	Coy in rest. Guns tested on improvised range among sand dunes S. of Camp. Unknown and T.A. in the afternoon.	WV
"	22.	8 a.m. 9 a.m. -noon	Physical Drill. Elementary and Advanced Gun Drill. Practice in making Offensive and Defensive Range Cards.	WV
"	23.	9 a.m.	Route march — LA PANNE — ADINKERKE — FURNES — COXYDE. Afternoon — Gun and Limber cleaning.	WV
"	24.		Forenoon — Church Parade. 44 Men (11 per Battalion of the Brigade) are attached permanently to the Coy. from this date, increasing total of attached men to 64. Several of the men sent were inefficient, and had to be exchanged. Class for these men started this afternoon.	WV
"	25.		Forenoon — Physical Drill. Demonstration of Ranging and Close Grouping Fire on Sea at LA PANNE BAINS. Shooting was very good, and observation excellent. Instruction class for attached men continued in the afternoon.	WV

WAR DIARY
or
INTELLIGENCE SUMMARY.

(Erase heading not required.)

Army Form C. 2118.

Place	Date	Hour	Summary of Events and Information	Remarks and references to Appendices
COXYDE (CAMP "JEAN BART")	June 1917 26	7 p.m.	Forenoon — Physical Drill, Gun Drill, Elementary and Advanced Instructional Class for men attached from Baths at Camp. Afternoon — Lt. J.B. NEILSON rejoined Coy from leave to U.K. "A" and "D" Sections were attached to 97th M.G. Coy. and proceeded into the line to positions E. of NIEUPORT. (Ref. Trench Maps BELGIUM Sheet 12 S.W. 1/20,000 M.29.)	WM
"	27.		Forenoon — Coy (less 2 Sections A and D) marched to shore at LA PANNE BAINS. Practice of Traversing Fire, Vertical Searching, and Combined Barrage Work. Afternoon — Mechanism from 2p.m. till 3p.m. and Instructional Class for attached men continued.	WM
"	28.		Forenoon — Short Route March, via COXYDE — FURNES — OOST DUNKERKE — COXYDE. Afternoon — Instructional Class continued. I.A. in billets. Heavy thunderstorm at night.	WM
"	29.		Forenoon — Inspection of all Gun Emplacements. Visual Training and Judging Distance on dunes behind Camp. Instruction Class continued. Afternoon — Mechanism and I.A. from 2p.m. to 3.15 p.m.	WM
"	30.		Heavy rainstorms during the night and rain all forenoon made work out of doors impossible. Gun Drill, Mechanism and Stoppages carried out in billets. Instructional Class continued. 2/Lt. SMITH joined Company from M.G. BASE. H.F. Williams Lt. GARDNER rejoined Company from M.G. SCHOOL. O.C. 196 M.G. Coy	WM

A 8534 Wt. W4973/M687 750,000 8/16 D.D. & L. Ltd. Forms/C.2118/13

WAR DIARY
or
INTELLIGENCE SUMMARY.
(Erase heading not required.)

Army Form C. 2118.

No 17

War Diary

96th Machine Gun Company

Volume XVII.

July 1st — July 31st

H.W. Williams Capt.
O.C. 96th Mn. G. Coy

in field 1.8.17

Place	Date	Hour	Summary of Events and Information	Remarks and references to Appendices

WAR DIARY
or
INTELLIGENCE SUMMARY.

(Erase heading not required.)

Army Form C. 2118.

Place	Date	Hour	Summary of Events and Information	Remarks and references to Appendices
COXYDE. (Camp JEAN BART.)	July 1917. 1.	11 a.m.	Church service in commemoration of the "Battle of the Somme" 1st July, 1916. No parades in the afternoon.	
		10 p.m.	"A" and "D" Sections were relieved from their line positions by sections of 219 M.G. Coy., and returned to billets in COXYDE.	
"	2.	9 a.m.	"B" and "C" Sections were attached to infantry battalions (2 guns to each battalion) in practice attack on LOMBARTZYDE, held in vicinity of GHYVELDE (Ref. Map 1:50,000 OSTEND). Guns went forward with 4th wave, to assist in immediate consolidation, and break down counter-attacks.	
			"A" and "D" sections stood in billets, and cleaned up, generally. Instruction Class for backward men was held from 9 a.m. to 12.15 p.m. and 2 p.m. to 4.15 p.m.	
"	3.	9 a.m.	Yesterday's programme repeated as regards "B" and "C" Sections, and Instruction Class. Remainder of Company went a route march. — COXYDE - FURNES - OOST DUNKERQUE - COXYDE. Only Instruction Class paraded in the afternoon.	
"	4.	9 a.m.	Company route march - (new) LA PANNE - ADENKERQUE - COXYDE. Afternoon. Complete Inspection and completion of Gas Appliances. Preparation of all guns, gun stores etc. for return to the line.	
"	5.		Forenoon - Physical drill: Paraded under section officers arrangements for complete inspection of section prior to going into the line. Afternoon Limber packing.	
H.Q. at NIEUPORT. Company in the line.	6.	8.30 p.m.	Company relieved 14th M.G. Coy. in the line, in sector between LOMBARTZYDE and ST GEORGES}. Ref. Map 1:20,000 BELGIUM 12 S.W. "B" Section Right : Found "A" Section Right : Reserve. "C" Section Left : Found "D" Section Left : Reserve. (Appsm). Map References: right : will no casualties. All relief complete by midnight. "A" Sect M36b; "B" Sect M31b. "C" Sect M30b. "D" Sect M29d and M30c.	

Army Form C. 2118.

WAR DIARY
or
INTELLIGENCE SUMMARY.
(Erase heading not required.)

Instructions regarding War Diaries and Intelligence Summaries are contained in F. S. Regs. Part II. and the Staff Manual respectively. Title pages will be prepared in manuscript.

Place	Date	Hour	Summary of Events and Information	Remarks and references to Appendices
Coy in line H.Q. at	July 1917 7		*Coy in the line. ST. GEORGES shelled during afternoon. Intermittent shelling of NIEUPORT. No casualties. Weather dull but warm.	* 12 men per Section in reserve at COXYDE.
NIEUPORT.	8	6 p.m.	Coy in the line. Weather excellent, and day fairly quiet. "B" Section guns moved back from front line positions to new Indoor Fire Emplacements were made. NIEUPORT heavily shelled. One casualty at H.Q.	
"	9.		Guns rearranged into "Group" System. Two "C" Section guns moved back from front line position to positions in M.36.b. Groups are now as follows:— No 1 Group. "A" Section and ½ "C" Section. No 2 Group. "B" Section No 3 Group. "D" Section and ½ "C" Section.	
H.Q. at FARM in M.32.d.			Coy H.Q. moved from NIEUPORT to FARM in M.32.d.	
"	10.		Intense hostile bombardment all along front from ST GEORGES to the sea. Enemy attacked on 97th Bde. (on our right) and 1st Division (Jaske left) fronts, capturing 1st and 2nd lines of 97th Bde, and during 1st Division advance across ISER River. Company fired 10,000 rounds during night of 10/11 to assist price on captured trenches by 16th LANC. FUS. Raid was unsuccessful. Signaller Corpl. PAWLEY recommended for Military Medal, as only Coy alone kept in communication with Brigade.	
"	11		Heavy enemy shelling continues but gradually slackening. H.Q. of Nos 1 and 2 groups (M.30.c.20.25) destroyed by shell fire, but no casualties. Coy fired 15,000 rounds on LOMBARTZYDE on night of 11/12 in response to S.O.S. Signal on that front.	

A 5831 Wt. W4973/MG57 750,000 8/16 D. D. & L. Ltd. Forms/C.2118/13.

WAR DIARY
or
INTELLIGENCE SUMMARY.
(Erase heading not required.)

Army Form C. 2118.

Place	Date July 1917	Hour	Summary of Events and Information	Remarks and references to Appendices
Cy on line H.Q. at Farm in M32d	12.		Find much quiet; but shelling shell columns, especially of canal bridges. Two "C" Section guns moved back from M30b to positions in M35b, and placed under No 2 Group. Cy "Stood to" all night; but nothing unusual happened. 2000 rounds fired at aircraft.	
"	13		Ordinary trench routine. Nothing unusual occurred on our front. 1500 rounds fired at aircraft. LT. G.F. GARDNER joined Coy from Tn G Base.	
"	14.		Ordinary trench routine. Artillery activity increased towards mid-night.	
"	15.		From 1 a.m. till 3 a.m. Coy fired 12,000 rounds on LOMBARTZYDE in support of attack by 114th Bde. Only guns of B and C Sections fired. The attack failed. Heavy rain fell during early hours of the morning.	
"	16		Ordinary trench routine. Our artillery continues to register on activity. No unusual event occurred. CAPT COOK attached to Coy from 219 M.S.Coy.	
"	17		Officers of 146th M.S.Coy visited gun positions today to reconnoitre in preparation for relief. Day passed very quietly.	
"	18.		Preparation for relief completed. New way out through Belgian lines reconnoitred to facilitate quick relief. New S.O.S. lines ordered by divn. and est. adj. on fresh range cards. 2/LT. OWEN joined Coy from M.S. Base.	

Army Form C. 2118.

WAR DIARY
or
INTELLIGENCE SUMMARY.
(Erase heading not required.)

Instructions regarding War Diaries and Intelligence Summaries are contained in F. S. Regs., Part II. and the Staff Manual respectively. Title pages will be prepared in manuscript.

Place	Date	Hour	Summary of Events and Information	Remarks and references to Appendices
Coyde Bains. H.Q. at FARM in M 32 d.	19.	9.30 p.m.	Coy relieved by 141st M.G. Coy. Relief completed at 12.30 a.m. on 20th. Section marched independently to billets in camp JEANNIOL, COXYDE, which they reached about 3 a.m. morning of 20th. No casualties during relief.	
COXYDE — COXYDE BAINS.	20.	2 p.m. 8 p.m.	Coy rested in the forenoon. Coy marched to billets in COXYDE BAINS. Ref map 1/40,000 OSTEND. Coy relieved 204 M.S. Coy in coast defences. 14 Guns Regimental, 4 to men per gun team. Defence sector stretches from NIEUPORT BAINS to ST IDESBALD. Relief completed 11.30 p.m. Remainder of Coy at rest in COXYDE BAINS.	
COXYDE BAINS.	21.		LT. GARDNER on leave to U.K. 14 Guns still occupied on coast defence. Remainder of Coy spent the day "cleaning up". Instructional Class recommenced with two guns & backward men.	
"	22	9.30 a.m. 11 a.m.	Church Parade at COXYDE BAINS. One O.R. admitted whilst bathing in the sea at ST. IDESBALD.	
"	23	9 a.m.	14 Guns still occupied on coast defence. Instruction Class continued 9 a.m. to 12.15 p.m. Remainder of the Company went on Route march via ST IDESBALD and COXYDE. Weather is very hot.	

WAR DIARY or INTELLIGENCE SUMMARY

Army Form C. 2118.

Place	Date	Hour	Summary of Events and Information	Remarks and references to Appendices
COXYDE BAINS	24		14 Guns still in Coast Defence. Remainder of Coy. employed under section Officers. Instruction Class as usual. LT HAMILTON to Hospital.	
"	25		Coast defence work. Rest of Company employed on Limber Cleaning and various training.	
"	26	5 p.m.	Coast defence work. COXYDE BAINS shelled slightly. No casualties.	
"	27	4.15 p.m. to 6 p.m. to 10 p.m.	Half Coy. marched from COXYDE BAINS to tents in BRAY DUNES PLAGE. Rif. Insp. 10ttrs OSTEND. Half Coy on Coast defence relieved by 219th M.G Coy, and proceeded to billets in COXYDE BAINS. No Casualties during relief. H.Q. moved to BRAY DUNES PLAGE.	
BRAY DUNES PLAGE.	28.	10 a.m.	Half Coy. marched from COXYDE BAINS to BRAY DUNES PLAGE. Remainder of Day Spent 'cleaning up'.	
"	29.	9 a.m. 10 a.m. 11 a.m.	21st Instalment on leave to U.K. Church Parade at BRAY DUNES PLAGE. Heavy Rain in afternoon. Limber cleaning in the afternoon, and Inspection of all gun appliances by Bde. gas N.C.O.	
"	30.		Inspection of Kit Equipment, Gun Stores etc. under Section Officers arrangements. Afternoon — Limber cleaning and packing. LT. S.F. GARDNER to "Aeroplane Course at BRAY DUNES.	
OUST DUNKERQUE (Camp 90).	31	6.15 a.m.	Coy. marched from BRAY DUNES PLAGE to OUST DUNKERQUE, Camp 90: Rif. Insp. tours OSTEND Reached billets 11 a.m. Rest during remainder of day.	

H Williams Cpt
O.C 96 M.G.Coy

No. 96 MACHINE GUN COMPANY.
No. 9
Date. 20.7.17

96th M.G. Coy Relief Orders

(1) 96th M.G. Coy. will relieve 20th M.G. Coy. in Coast Defence on the night 20th/21st July.

(2) The Coast will be divided into 4 Sectors, & Sections will be allotted as follows
   - NIEUPORT SECTOR — "A" Section — 4 guns
   - OOST DUNKIRKE " — "B" " — 4 "
   - COXYDE " — "D" " — 4 "
   - ST IDESBALDE — "C" " — 2 "

(3) Detachments of Sections going into the line will be commanded by the following Officers.
   - "A" ---------- Lieut. G.F. Gardner
   - "B" ---------- 2/Lieut. C.H. Smith
   - "D" ---------- 2/Lieut. G.P. Owens
   - "C" ---------- 2/Lieut. C.S. Grimsley

(4) Sections will parade outside Coy. H.Q. at 9 P.M. in the order as given above, with one limber per section.

(5) (a) Eight belt boxes per gun will be taken.
    (b) Sections will be rationed till to-morrow night.
    (c) Dress:- Battle order.

(6) Guides from 20th Coy will be at 96th M.G. Coy. H.Q. at 9 PM to take sections to their position.
    One H.Q. guide 96th M.G. Coy will go with each Section to bring back report of relief complete.

Copies to :-
1. O.C. 96th M.G. Coy.
2-5. 4 Sections
6. Transport Officer
7. File
8-9. War Diary
10. H.Q. Section
11. C.S.M.

H.H. Williams Capt
96th Machine Gun Company

No. 96 MACHINE GUN COMPANY.
No. 3
Date 26.7.17

Copy No. 12

96th M.G. Coy. Relief Orders.

(1) 96th M.G. Coy is being relieved in the Coast Defences by 214 M.G. Coy on July 27th.

(2) Sections will be relieved as follows:-
    NIEUPORT SECTION at 4.30 P.M.
    OOST DUNKIRKE "   " "   "
    COXYDE   "   " 6   P.M.
    St IDESBALDE   "   " "   "

(3) H.Q. Guides will be provided at Coy. H.Q. to take relieving sections to Section H.Q in the line.
    Sections will be responsible for guiding each relieving gun team to its proper position.

(4) H.Q. Guides will be ready at Coy H.Q. to take sections of 214 M.G. Coy to their respective positions.
    For NIEUPORT SECTION at 5.30 P.M
      " OOST DUNKIRKE   "   " 6.15 "
      " COXYDE   "   " 5.30 "
      " St IDESBALDE   "   " 5.30 "

(5) All maps, plans & defence schemes will be handed over. Section Officers will explain carefully nature of work in progress.

(6) On relief Sections of 96th M.G. Coy will march to billets in COXYDE BAINS.

(7) ACKNOWLEDGE.

H.H. Williams Capt.
Comdg 96th M.G. Coy

Copies to:-

1)
2-5.) Station Commanders
6.) 46th Inf. Bde
7.) 144 Inf. Bde
8.) Transport Officer 96th M.G.C.
9.) 214 M.G. Coy.
10.) C.S.M. 96 M.G. Coy
11-12.) War Diary
13.) File
14.) Officers for information

Issued at 9 p.m.

20.7.17.

Army Form C. 2118.

WAR DIARY
or
INTELLIGENCE SUMMARY.
(Erase heading not required.)

96/18

96th MG Company

WAR DIARY

August 1st – 31st

1917

Vol 18

H Williams Cpt.
Comd 96. M. Co. Cy

Army Form C. 2118.

WAR DIARY
or
INTELLIGENCE SUMMARY.
(Erase heading not required.)

Instructions regarding War Diaries and Intelligence Summaries are contained in F.S. Regs., Part II. and the Staff Manual respectively. Title pages will be prepared in manuscript.

Month: **August, 1917**

Place	Date	Hour	Summary of Events and Information	Remarks and references to Appendices
OOST DUNKIRKE	1st		In camp at OOST DUNKIRKE. Very heavy rain.	14th
"	2nd		In camp. Moved up to the ST GEORGE'S SECTOR, but whilst on the march orders were received cancelling relief.	14th
"	3rd		Relieved 146th M.G. Coy in ST GEORGE'S SECTOR. Relief complete 12 m.n. Casualties nil; no unusual shelling. 16 guns in the line.	14th
In the Line	4th		In the line. Eight guns were employed on HARASSING FIRE, various tangles to the enemy's defences being selected. About 30,000 rounds per day were fired.	14th
ST GEORGE'S SECTOR	6th			
	7th to 9th		Raid by 16th N.F. BATTALIONS 1-40 A.M. on night 7/8th on RAT TRENCH. Probable barrage was put down, about 35,000 rounds being fired; 4 men wounded. On the night of 8/9th a Projector Gas Attack was launched on GRISETTE BAIN BURGH Pn. In conjunction with this we fired 22,000 on various tangles from 1-30 A.M. – 4-0 A.M. In addition to this about 25,000 – 30,000 rounds were fired each 24 hours.	14th

WAR DIARY
or
INTELLIGENCE SUMMARY.

(Erase heading not required.)

Army Form C. 2118.

August, 1917

Place	Date	Hour	Summary of Events and Information	Remarks and references to Appendices
In the Line	10th		Guns fired about 20,000 rounds harassing fire, and 17,000 rounds in response to S.O.S. signals from LOMBARTZYDE SECTOR at 9.0 P.M. - 9.30 P.M.	Uth
	11th to 15th		Guns employed on harassing fire daily. On the 12th at 4.30 P.M. 6 men were wounded by shell fire on the BRUGES ROAD. Enemy shelled back areas fairly constantly	Uth
	16th		At 1.30 A.M. a Projector Gas Attack was launched on 49th Divisional Sector; our guns fired 16,000 rounds in conjunction	Uth
	17th		About 8,600 fired on various targets. In all during the low about 300,000 rounds were fired by day & night guns. Observation throughout the town was poor — the weather dull & wet	Uth
	18th & 19th		Relieved in the line by 98th M.G. Coy. Relief complete by 11.20 P.M. Sections marched to billets in COXYDE. About 10 A.M. Company marched to billets at BRAY DUNES PLAGE	Uth

Army Form C. 2118.

WAR DIARY
or
INTELLIGENCE SUMMARY.
(Erase heading not required.)

Instructions regarding War Diaries and Intelligence Summaries are contained in F.S. Regs., Part II. and the Staff Manual respectively. Title pages will be prepared in manuscript.

Place	Date	Hour	Summary of Events and Information	Remarks and references to Appendices
BRAY DUNES PLAGE	20th		In billets. Time was spent in cleaning up, refitting, and training. Men were taught the new methods of Bayonet Drill & A.A. work.	
	16		On 26th the Company was organised into two batteries each of two sections. Lieut S.B. NEILSON was appointed Battery Commander of No 1, and Lieut D Gardner of No 2. These batteries were administered as units under the control of the Company Commander.	Itd
	27th			
COXYDE	28th		Marched to COXYDE. Very heavy rain. Enemy shelled AUSTRALIA CAMP from 1 P.M. onwards — two men wounded. Company moved into bivouacs in X 13 c.	Itd
	29th		In bivouacs — usual training was carried out	
	16			
	31st		Weather dull & rainy	Itd

Hawthorne Capt
Comd. 96 M.G. Coy

96th M.G. Coy. Operation Order   Copy No 9

1.) The 96th Inf. Bde. is carrying out a raid on RAT POST, RAT TRENCH on — night

2.) The 96th M.G. Coy. will assist by putting up a barrage on the enemy's trench system in N14.

3.) For the purpose of the raid the guns of 96th M.G. Coy. will be divided as follows:
   - No. 1 Group   6 guns "B" Sect. + 2 guns "D" Sect
   - " 2 "   4 " "A" Section
   - " 3 "   4 " "C" "
   - " 4 "   2 " "D" Sect. (less 2 guns)

4.) The barrage will be put down at Zero hour + will continue until Z+40 as follows:-
   All Groups
   - 0 to 0+10   at 150 rounds a min.
   - 0+10 to 0+20   at 50 " " "
   - 0+20 to 0+30   at 100 " " "
   - 0+30 to 0+40   at 50 " " "

   At Zero +40 guns will be laid on the defensive lines at present in use.

5.) Targets will be allotted to Groups as follows:-
   - No 1 Group to fire on lines N14a 35,25 — N19c 90,70
   - No 2   " { 2 guns on N19c 35,10
                 { 2 " " N14c 40,10
   - No 3   " { 2 " " N14a 40,65
              { 1 " " N14b 10,1
              { 1 " " N14b 20,15

   No 4 GROUP 2 guns NIEUWENDAMME FORT N20c 10,45

6.) No I group will cover the whole _____ _____

_____ _____ _____ _____

7.) R.S.B. _____ _____
Group Commanders will return a copy _____ to Coy by
tomorrow morning post

8.) Instructions as to positions of D.S. (at 200 x paces) are
being issued separately to O.C. "D" Section

9.) Zero day + hour will be notified later.

10.) ACKNOWLEDGE

H.T.Williams Capt.
O.C. 96th M.G. Coy.

issued at

Copies 6:-
   No.1. O.C. Company
     2. A. Section
     3. B. Section
     4. C. "
     5. D. "
     6. 2nd I/C for information
     7. 10th Inf Bde
     8. _____ War Diary
     9. _____
     10. _____

War Diary

96th M.G. Company Relief Order 4.   Copy No 71

1.) 96th M.G. Coy. is relieving 146th M.G. Coy in the ST GEORGES SECTOR to-night, 2nd/3rd August.

2.) Guides from 146 M.G. Coy will be at Coy H.Q. to mark Sections of 96 M.G. Coy. as follows:-
    8.30 P.M. ---------- "D" Section
    8.45 " ---------- "A"   "
    9.0 " ---------- "B"   "
    9.15 " ---------- "C"   "

3.) "D" Section will relieve a section of 146 M.G. Coy in M 36 B. The other three sections will be guided direct to the battle positions already prepared by 146 M.G. Coy.

4.) Great care must be taken to ensure that guns are laid at once on defensive lines. All figures and calculations received will be carefully checked.

5.) 146 M.G. Coy will hand over tripods & eight belt boxes per gun, also pivot mountings, anti-aircraft sights & all maps & documents. Receipts will be given.

6.) Sections will be organised as laid down and two complete gun teams per section will be left at the Transport lines.

7.) Belt boxes will be made up to 8 boxes per gun.

8.) H.Q. Guide will be attached to each Section to bring back report of relief complete.

9.) Coy H.Q. will be established at M 32 D 05.14

(10.) ACKNOWLEDGE.

Field 2-5-17.

Issued at 3.15 pm

Copies to:-

1.) O.C.
2 - 5.) in Sections
6.) Transport Officer 96th M.G. Coy
7.) O.C. 146 M.G. Coy
8.) 46th Inf Bde.
9.) C.S.M. 96th M.G. Coy
10.) H.Q. Wing Diary.
11.) File.

H H Williams Capt.,
O.C. 96th M.G. Coy

96th M.G. Coy. Relief Order No 21   Copy No. 12

1) 96th M.G Coy is being relieved by 98th M.G. Coy in the St George's Sector on the night 18th/19th August.

2) For the purpose of relief, guns of 96th M.G. Coy will be divided in 3 Groups
    No. 1 Group   "D" Section
    No. 2   "   "A"   "
    No. 3   "   "B.C" "

3) 98th M.G. Coy is only putting 12 guns in the line as under
    No. 1 Group   4 guns
    " 2   "   4   "
    " 3   "   4   " (B Sect provisional)

Note. Guns of No.3 Group not being 4 these will withdraw simultaneously with the other guns of the group.

4) Sections of 98th M.G. Coy will arrive at PELICAN BRIDGE at the following times.
    To relieve No 1 Group   8.30 p.m
    "   "   No 2 "   8.45 "
    "   "   No 3 "   9.0   "

5) One H.Q. guide for each Group will be at PELICAN BRIDGE to guide relieving sections to Group H.Qs where they will be met by 1 guide per gun.

6) All belt boxes, A.A. pivot mountings, trench mountings, maps, defence schemes will be handed over & receipts taken.
A.A. Sights & "Z" Barrage schemes will not be handed over.

7.) Limbers for sections of 96th M.G.Coy will be on the WIEDTZ BAR PONTOON BRIDGE. There will be one limber per Section. The [?] section will have the first limber on the road.
Limbers will be on the WILLPEN ROAD at [?] P.M.
One limber guide to be at Coy Hd.Qrs at 8:30 p.m.

8.) Relief complete will be reported through 45th M.G.Coy.

9.) On completion of relief sections will march to billets in O.o.C DIOCLETIAN via WILLPEN

10.) ACKNOWLEDGE

H.F. Williams Capt.,
O.C. 96th Machine Gun Company

Copies to:-
 1. O.C. 46th M.G.Coy
 2. O.C. A Section
 3. O.C. B "
 4. O.C. C "
 5. O.C. D "
 6. 14th Inf. Bde
 7. T.O. 96th M.G.Coy
 8. " 45th -do-
 9. " 46th -do-
 10. R.O.
 War Diary

Army Form C. 2118.

WAR DIARY
or
INTELLIGENCE SUMMARY.
(Erase heading not required.)

96th M.G. Company

War Diary

for

September, 1917

Vol XIX

H Williams Capt
Com'g 96 M G Cy

1/10/17

Army Form C. 2118.

WAR DIARY
or
INTELLIGENCE SUMMARY.

(Erase heading not required.)

SEPTEMBER 1917

Instructions regarding War Diaries and Intelligence Summaries are contained in F. S. Regs. Part II. and the Staff Manual respectively. Title pages will be prepared in manuscript.

Place	Date	Hour	Summary of Events and Information	Remarks and references to Appendices
AUSTRALIA CAMP LE g COXYDE	1/9/17		Company in bivouacs, weather showery. Forenoon:- Coy training, anti aircraft defence of Camp. Afternoon:- Recreation. Camp entries during night.	
— do —	2/9/17		Weather fine. Forenoon:- Church parade	
— do —	3/9/17	11 a.m.	Weather bright & hot. G.O.C. inspected the Camp. Company practised new "Barrage Drill" by Bettaine. Afternoon:- Recreation & Kit inspection by Section Officers	
— do —	4/9/17		Weather bright & hot. Forenoon:- Gun tests on stor at W10a, Capt. Williams on leave to U.K. Capt. J.O. Cook temporarily in command of Coy. Afternoon:- Recreation, inspection of ironwork, Gas appliances etc.	
— do —	5/9/17	9·15 p.m.	Weather bright & hot. Forenoon:- 2/Lt. R.H.L. Griffith returned from leave to U.K. E.Y. elementary Gun drill & barrage drill. Lecture on Anti aircraft work. Afternoon:- Brigade Sports. Camp bombed by aircraft.	
— do —	6/9/17		Heavy Thunderstorm in early morning. Forenoon:- Route march, St. Idesbald - Furnes - Coyg D. Transport inspected by O.C. Du Ta. Afternoon:- Brigade football tournament.	

Army Form C. 2118.

WAR DIARY
or
INTELLIGENCE SUMMARY.
(Erase heading not required.)

Instructions regarding War Diaries and Intelligence Summaries are contained in F. S. Regs., Part II. and the Staff Manual respectively. Title pages will be prepared in manuscript.

Place	Date	Hour	Summary of Events and Information	Remarks and references to Appendices
AUSTRALIA CAMP	Sept 1917 7	Forenoon	Plenuntary Gun Drill + Barrage Drill.	W/
		Afternoon	Research. Enemy aeroplane when over the Camp at night	
"	8	Forenoon	Barrage Drill. Anti-aircraft Lecture and drill	W/
		Afternoon	Football	
"	9		Church Parade 9 a.m. 10.30 a.m. 11 a.m. in CANADA CAMP.	W/
"	10		Company employed in working parties at HULL DUMP, between COXYDE and OUST DUNKERQUE. Training Suspended. Weather still fine.	W/
"	11	Forenoon	Limber cleaning and checking of Stores preparatory to going into the line.	W/
		2 p.m.	Afternoon - Inspection of Transport by the G.O.C.	
"	12	7 a.m.	Forenoon - C.O. and Battery Commander reconnoitred the M.G. positions in the LOMBARTZYDE Sector of the line. Company employed on Barrage drill. Enemy aircraft were again very active at night, dropping bombs in the vicinity of the Camp. No Casualties were caused.	W/

WAR DIARY
or
INTELLIGENCE SUMMARY.

Army Form C. 2118.

Place	Date Sept 1917	Hour	Summary of Events and Information	Remarks and references to Appendices
Company in the line H.Q. @ NIEUPORT M34.a.8.6.	13.		Famous — Enemy fairly quiet. LT W.S. ELIAS on leave to U.K.	
		6.30 p.m	Coy relieved 14th M.G. Coy in LOMBARTZYDE Section R/Map 20,000 LOMBARTZYDE. A Section in M29.c.d. } 1 M.G. gun each in A.A. work. B " " M28.c. C & D Sections in THE REDAN, M28.a and M28.b. Relief completed w/t no casualties, by 9.30 p.m. Transport remains at COXYDE. 8 Guns are employed on S.O.S. work and 8 on CLOSE DEFENCE.	✓
		10.45 p/m	Company guns fired in LOMBARTZYDE in support of Pagschle Gas attack, in all 18,000 rounds.	
	14		Coy in the line. The REDAN to heavily shelled from time to time, and the bridges and Henies things are quiet and the usual Trench Routine prevails. Harassing fire is carried out daily by A and B Sections — Total rounds fired each day = 8,000.	✓
	15			
	16			
	17	6 a.m.	S.O.S. signal went up on LOMBARTZYDE front at 6 a.m. all S.O.S. guns of the Company fired till the Situation cleared, in all 30,000 rounds. (Harassing fire in addition.) The weather still continues excellent. 31392 PTE. BRENNAN recommended for Military Medal for courageous gun work under heavy shell fire.	✓
			70327 PTE R. SUMMERBELL recommended for Military Medal for excellent work during S.O.S. barrage. 44791 PTE. C. GRIFFITHS recommended for Military medal for excellent work as B.Coy. runner on same occasion.	✓

Army Form C. 2118.

WAR DIARY
or
INTELLIGENCE SUMMARY.
(Erase heading not required.)

Instructions regarding War Diaries and Intelligence Summaries are contained in F. S. Regs., Part II. and the Staff Manual respectively. Title pages will be prepared in manuscript.

Place	Date	Hour	Summary of Events and Information	Remarks and references to Appendices
Coy in the LINE	18 19 20 21		Coy still in the line. Weather excellent. Wind following from easterly direction. One of our A.A. guns assisted in bringing down an enemy aeroplane on evening of 21st. Nothing else of importance occurred during these days.	W
"	22.	2pm	One C Sectⁿ gun destroyed by shell fire in the REDAN at M.28.a.62.7. 1 O.R. Killed and 2 Wounded.	W
	23 24 25 26		Usual Trench Routine. Capt. WILLIAMS returned from leave to U.K. on 24th and resumed Command of Company. Capt. COOK returned to transport lines. On evening of 26th enemy sent over cloud gas. 1 O.R. was gassed in the REDAN.	W
	27.	6am	S.O.S. Signal went up on LOMBARTZYDE sector, and all S.O.S guns fired an S.O.S. line. Total Rounds fired 23,000. Coy H.Q. in NIEUPORT was shelled heavily during the day, two direct hits on shelter obtaining direct hits. 4 O.R. were gassed, two of them severely.	W

WAR DIARY
or
INTELLIGENCE SUMMARY.
(Erase heading not required.)

Army Form C. 2118.

Place	Date	Hour	Summary of Events and Information	Remarks and references to Appendices
In the line	28	—	Usual Trench Routine. List of recommendations for New Year Honours made out:— LT. J.B. NEILSON recommended for M.C LT D GARDINER 7748 SGT BELL } Mention in dispatches. 7753 SGT WRATTEN Coy. S.M. SHERWOOD	W
"	29	6 p.m.	Coy relieved by Section of 97th M.G. Coy. Relief complete with no casualties by 9.15 p.m. On relief Section marched to bivouac in AUSTRALIA CAMP, COXYDE; being finally settled by midnight.	W
AUSTRALIA CAMP. COXYDE.	30.		Church Parades. (1) Fatigue party of 57 O.R. provided for work at HULL DUMP. Three guns mounted for A.A. defence of the Sector. Otherwise No parades.	W

H A Williams Capt
O.C. 96 M.G.Coy

96th. MACHINE GUN COMPANY RELIEF ORDERS No. 38   Coy.No. 9

1. The 96th.M.G.Coy. is relieving 14th.M.G.Coy. in the LOMBARTZYDE SECTOR to-night 13/14 September.

2. Guns will be distributed as follows:-
   Left Group   Nos. 1.2.3. & 4.
   "B" Section, No.1 Battery. 2/Lieut. Smith in command.

   Centre Group   Nos. 8. 9.10.11.12.5.6.7.
   No.2 Battery less 1 gun. Lieut. D.Gardiner in command.

   Right Group   No. 3.13.14.15.16.
   "A" Section No.1 Battery and 1 gun No.2 Battery, Lieut. G.F.Gardner in command.

3. Guides from 14th.M.G.Coy. will be at Arch Bridge, NIEUPORT to meet Sections at the following times :-
      "A" Section .... 6.30 p.m.
      "B"   "   .... 6.30 "
      "C"   "   .... 6.45 "
      "D"   "   .... 7.0   "

4. Gun teams will consist of 1 N.C.O. and 4 men. Two complete gun teams per Section will be left at the Transport lines.

5. A carrying party of 2 men per gun team under charge of Sgt. Jones will be detailed by Battery Commanders to help carrying in.
   On completion of relief these men will be guided back to Coy.H.Q. by H.Q.Runner attached to each. They will then be marched back to COXYDE by Sgt.Jones.

6. All maps, plans, aeroplane photographs and all trench stores will be taken over and carefully checked, proper receipts will be given.

7. The 14th.M.G.Coy.will hand over 16 belt boxes per gun.

8. All calculations, gun positions etc.will be carefully checked and reported upon by Group Commanders and guns laid at once on their S.O.S. lines.

9. H.Q.Guides will be attached to each Group for purpose of reporting relief complete.

10. Coy.H.Q.will be established at M 34 c 75.75.

11. Reliefs are to be reported complete by 9.45 p.m.

    ACKNOWLEDGE.

                                              J.C.Cock.
                                                     Capt.,
                                       O.C. 96th.Machine Gun Company.

   Issued at........
   Copies to:-
     1. O/C.
   2-5. 4 Sections
     6. Transport Officer 96th.M.G.Coy.
     7. O/C. 14th.M.G.Coy.
     8. 96th. Infantry Brigade
   9-10. War Diary
     11. File

Field 13.9.17

Copy No........ 11

96th. M.G.Coy. RELIEF ORDER No.25

1. 96th.M.G.Coy. is being relieved in the LOMBARTZYDE SECTOR on the night 29th/30th. by 97th.M.G.Coy.

2. Defence Schemes, Lines of Fire, Range Charts, Belt boxes, and all Trench stores taken over on coming into the line, will be handed over and receipts taken.

3. Guns will be relieved in the following order:-
    No. 2 Battery   8 guns   REDAN
    "A" Section   4 "   YSER CANAL
    "B"   "   4 "   NEW PARADE

4. Incoming sections will be at T shape ZOUAVE Rd. at the following times:-
    For No.2 Battery
        1st. Section   at 6.30 p.m.
        2nd.   "   " 6.45 "
    For "A" Section   " 7.0   "
      " "B"   "   " 7.15 "

5. Guides will be there in time to take them to Battery and Section Hd.Qrs. Great care will be taken that there are sufficient guides to take relieving teams to guns of No.2 Battery.

6. Arrangements for Limbers of 96th. M.G.Coy. will be as follows:-
    No.2. Battery   1 Limber at 9.0 p.m. at junction of BRUGES & RAMSCAPELLE Rds.
    "A" Section   1 Limber at 9.15 p.m. at the same place.
    "B"   "   1 Limber at 9.0 p.m. at PELICAN BRIDGE on VULPEN Rd.

7. Relief complete will be reported to Coy H.Q. through messengers of relieving Company.

8. On completion of relief sections will march independently to bivouaces at COXYDE? where tea will be provided.

9. H.Q. Limber will be at Coy. H.Q.at 6.15 p.m.

10. 97th. M.G.Coy. will send in 1 N.C.O. or man per gun 24 hours before relief. These will be guided to their respective Hd.Qrs. by the ration parties on the 28th. They should be given all information possible about the line.

11. ACKNOWLEDGE

Capt.,
O.C. 96th. Machine Gun Company

Copies to
1. O.C.
2.&3. O.C. No.1 Battery 96th.M.G.Coy.
4 "5. "   " 2   "   "
6. 2nd in Command   "
7. Transport Officer   "
8. 96th. Inf. Bde.
9. 97th. M.G.Coy.
10. Quartermaster 96th. M.G.Coy.
11.)
12.) War Diary

WAR DIARY
or
INTELLIGENCE SUMMARY.

Army Form C. 2118.

Vol 20

War Diary
96th M.G.C.
Vol XX
October, 1917

H.T. Williams Capt
Comdg 96 M G Coy

WAR DIARY
or
INTELLIGENCE SUMMARY.
(Erase heading not required.)

Army Form C. 2118.

Place	Date	Hour	Summary of Events and Information	Remarks and references to Appendices
COYDE (Australian Camp)	Oct 1917 1	8.30am 12.30pm afternoon	Company in rest. Training. Recreation	The Camp & neighborhood shelled intermittently during the night, hostile planes over at night. Weather fine, fine flat.	H&L
"	2	8.30am 12.30pm afternoon	Company training Recreation	Hostile planes over at night. Weather fine, fine flat.	18th
"	3	8.30am 12.30pm afternoon	Company training Recreation	Weather fine, rain at night.	18th
"	4	"	Company training only partly carried out owing to rain. Private O'Malley tried by F.G.C.M.		18th
BRAY DUNES	5		Company moved from Camp at COYDE to Camp at BRAY DUNES. Wet		18th
"	6		Company training carried on in the huts owing to the rain. Captain J.O Cook went on leave to U.K.		—
"	7		Church service in forenoon, no parades in afternoon		18th
"	8	8.30 am 12.30 pm afternoon	Company training Company Sports		18th

WAR DIARY
or
INTELLIGENCE SUMMARY.

(Erase heading not required.)

Army Form C. 2118.

Instructions regarding War Diaries and Intelligence Summaries are contained in F.S. Regs., Part II. and the Staff Manual respectively. Title pages will be prepared in manuscript.

Place	Date Oct.	Hour	Summary of Events and Information	Remarks and references to Appendices
BRAY DUNES	9	8.30am 12.30pm	Company training. Heavy rain at night. Dance in afternoon	181
"	10	"	Company training. Interbrigade special parade in full marching order for inspection & clothing requirement.	180
"	11	"	Company training. In the afternoon the Company was photographed.	181
"	12	"	Company training. In the afternoon – football	181
"	13	"	Captain Williams went on course at XIII Corps School. Lieut Doar Edittim temporarily in Command J Company.	181
"	14	8.30am 12.30pm 4.30pm	Company training in Lute swimp to bus workers. Church Service in forenoon. Two new Anti Aircraft mountings arrived for C/o Machine Gun Officer	181
"	15	8.30am 12.30am	Company training. Dance in afternoon	181

Army Form C. 2118.

WAR DIARY
INTELLIGENCE SUMMARY.
(Erase heading not required.)

Instructions regarding War Diaries and Intelligence Summaries are contained in F. S. Regs., Part II. and the Staff Manual respectively. Title pages will be prepared in manuscript.

Place	Date	Hour	Summary of Events and Information	Remarks and references to Appendices
BRAY DUNES	16	8·30 a.m. 12·30 p.m.	Company training & firing on Beach. Football in afternoon. Captn McMunn returned on leave. Captn J.B. Nelson went on leave to U.K.	H.Q.
"	17	8·30 a.m. 12·30 p.m.	Company training through fire on beach. Football in afternoon.	H.Q.
"	18	8·30 a.m. 12·30 p.m.	Company training. Firing on beach. Smoke clean up & ordinary Lewis Gun training stores in afternoon.	H.Q.
"	19	8·30 a.m. 4·0 p.m.	On forenoon rehearsed barrage demonstration with D.M.G.O. & 5 Guns of the Company along with 16 Guns of 217 Coy. & 6 Guns of 97 M. Coy. Barrage demonstration firing fire out to Sea. Captn J.O. Cook rejoined from leave.	H.Q.
"	20	8·30 a.m. 12·30 p.m.	Company training, cleaning up & musketry. Football in afternoon.	V
"	21		Church services in morning. Football in afternoon. Captain Williams completed 12 months in command of the Company.	H.Q.

Army Form C. 2118.

WAR DIARY
INTELLIGENCE SUMMARY.
(Erase heading not required.)

Instructions regarding War Diaries and Intelligence Summaries are contained in F.S. Regs., Part II. and the Staff Manual respectively. Title pages will be prepared in manuscript.

Place	Date	Hour	Summary of Events and Information	Remarks and references to Appendices
BRAY DUNES	22 Oct	8.30 am 12.30 pm	Company training. Football in afternoon	WR
"	23	8.30 am 12.30 pm	Company training in huts owing to bad weather	WR
"	24	8.30 am 12.30 pm	Company training, Lewis gun fire on beach	WR
TETEGHEM AREA	25	8.00 am	Company mov(ed) from Camp at BRAY DUNES to billets at FERME DU NORD, J.19.d & J.25.b. maps Belgium & (part of) France Sheet 19.	WR
ERINGHEM AREA	26		Company marched from billets at Ferme du Nord to billets in Eringhem area T.22 & T.23; map Belgium & part of France, April 19.	WR
"	27	8.30 am 12.30 pm	Company training. Football in afternoon	WR
"	28		Football in morning. Church Service & Football in afternoon	WR

Army Form C. 2118.

WAR DIARY
INTELLIGENCE SUMMARY.
(Erase heading not required.)

Instructions regarding War Diaries and Intelligence Summaries are contained in F. S. Regs., Part II. and the Staff Manual respectively. Title pages will be prepared in manuscript.

Place	Date	Hour	Summary of Events and Information	Remarks and references to Appendices
ERINGHEM AREA	29	6.30am 12.30pm	Company training. Football in afternoon. Lieut J.B. NEILSON returned from leave	
"	30	6.30am 12.30pm	Company training in fields owing to rain.	
"	31	9.0 am	Company paraded & marched to A.11.a. huts Belgium & Battn. Hqrs about 27 for inspection by G.O.C. 32nd Division at 12 noon. Football in afternoon	

H.W. Mason Capt
Cmdg 96th M.G.Cy

Army Form C. 2118.

WAR DIARY
or
INTELLIGENCE SUMMARY.
(Erase heading not required.)

Vol 21

WAR DIARY

96TH COY. MACHINE GUN CORPS.

VOL. 21.

all the enunk 2/4
for O.C. 96 Coy
96. M.G.C.

Army Form C. 2118.

WAR DIARY
or
INTELLIGENCE SUMMARY.

(Erase heading not required.)

Instructions regarding War Diaries and Intelligence Summaries are contained in F. S. Regs. Part II. and the Staff Manual respectively. Title pages will be prepared in manuscript.

Place	Date	Hour	Summary of Events and Information	Remarks and references to Appendices
Brighton Camp	Nov 1st	W.b.	Gun cleaning & short lectures in billets	(A.)(1)
hqrs 19 Inf brigade France 19 SN 2nd Edition 1/20,000	2nd	Forenoon Afternoon	Bayonet drill & physical training Cross country run	(A.)(1)
T 23 c	3rd	Forenoon Afternoon	Bayonet drill & physical training Lieut. G. F. GARDNER Inter-Section football. Leave to U.K.	(A.)(1)
—do—	4th	Forenoon Afternoon	Physical training, elementary gun drill. Arms drill. Inter-section football. Football competition	(A.)(1)
—do—	5th	Forenoon Afternoon	Physical drill, Arms drill. Gas defence drill Trial of water-section football competition	(A.)(1)
—do—	6th	Forenoon Afternoon	Physical training, 'I.A' & 'Stoppages' in billets owing to rain Cross country run	Captain J. J. Cook to CAMIERS for M.G. exam (A.)(1)
—do—	7th	Forenoon Afternoon	Physical training, 'Stoppages'. short lectures in billets owing to rain Football, Coy team v. no. 96 Bryant H.Q. team	(A.)(1)

WAR DIARY or INTELLIGENCE SUMMARY

Army Form C. 2118.

(Erase heading not required.)

Place	Date	Hour	Summary of Events and Information	Remarks and references to Appendices
Camp in Jarn area	Nov 8th	Forenoon	Company training	(A.) J.F.7
		Afternoon	Inter. Battery football	
do	9th	Forenoon	Men of Company had baths.	(A.) J.F.7
		Afternoon	Paper chase	
do	10th	Wet.	Gun cleaning & packing up ready for move tomorrow	(A.) J.F.7
Longuehut Jarn	11th		*Company marched into billets in Longuehut area FRANCE 27 N.W. Series "B" 2nd Edition C. 24 B	(A.) J.F.7
Winnizeele area	12th		*Company marched into billets in Winnizeele area FRANCE 27 N.W. Series "B" 2nd Edition C.12 D	(A.) J.F.7
WATOU area map reference Belgium & France Edition 2 1/40000 sheet 27 LC3	13th		Company marched to Schools Camp in Watou area, men all under canvas.	(A.) J.F.7
	14th	Forenoon	Physical training. Teams drill, improvements to the camp.	(A.) J.F.7
			Camp inspected by G.O.C. 32nd Division	
	15th	Forenoon	Physical training, arms drill & improvements to the Camp.	(A.) J.F.7
		6 pm - 8 pm	Night marching across country. 2/Lt. C.S. GRUNDY seen to U.K.	
do	16th	Forenoon	Physical training, Bayrs drill, Camp cleaning	(A.) J.F.7
			Camp inspected by Corps Commander	

WAR DIARY
or
INTELLIGENCE SUMMARY.

(Erase heading not required.)

Army Form C. 2118.

Place	Date	Hour	Summary of Events and Information	Remarks and references to Appendices
Watou area (Belg) Reg. 3rd R.R. France 2 Div. 2 Corps 2/IE 3C	Nov 17th	Forenoon	Physical training, Arms drill, Gas drill. Demonstration of use of Yukon stove under supervision of D.M.G.O, L.O.	(x.) (y)
	18th	Forenoon afternoon	Physical training. Church Services. Company baths	(x.) (y)
—do—	19th	Forenoon	Attack of Company went through Gas chamber. Physical training. Arms drill under Lieut G.V.E. GARDNER reported back from leave.	(x.) (y)
—do—	20th	Forenoon 5pm - 7.30pm	Physical training, Arms drill, Barrage drill. Four officers went to see model of IInd Corps front at Poperinghe. No. 2 Battery night manoeuvring	(x.) (y)
—do—	21st	Forenoon afternoon 5pm - 7.30pm	Physical training. Gas defence drill under Divisional Gas officer Runner + Signallers went to see mostly, IInd Corps front. No 1 Bttery - night ty - manoeuvring	(x.) (y)
—do—	22nd	Forenoon	Physical training, Barrage drill. Packing limbers. Commanding Officer + Battery Commanders went to reconnoitre 1st Divn front.	(x.) (y)

Army Form C. 2118.

WAR DIARY
or
INTELLIGENCE SUMMARY.
(Erase heading not required.)

Instructions regarding War Diaries and Intelligence Summaries are contained in F.S. Regs., Part II. and the Staff Manual respectively. Title pages will be prepared in manuscript.

Place	Date	Hour	Summary of Events and Information	Remarks and references to Appendices
DAMBRE CAMP Belgium 28 NW Edit: 6A - B 27 C 86	Nov 23rd		Company moved from Schools Camp to Dambre Camp.	(1) 17
-do-	24th	Forenoon	Physical training. Cleaning up the camp. Three Lewis Officers went to reconnoitre 1st Division front.	(2) 17
		Afternoon	Lewis gun officers & transport lines.	
-do-	25th	Forenoon	Physical Training & Small arms kit. Inspection. Wore anti-gas appliances.	(3) 17
-do-	26th	Forenoon	Physical training, and Lewis Gun & Transport lines. Company Officer & O.C. 2 Battery Commander went to reconnoitre the line with the D.A.L.O.	(4) 17
-do-	27th	Forenoon	Gun work & short lectures in huts owing to the rain.	(5) 17
		Afternoon	Packing up & filling up G.S. wheelers to going into line tomorrow.	
In the line Coy H.Q. KANSAS FARM (SPRIET map 1/10000)	28th		Company relieved 97th Coy A.M.S. Coy in the line. Coy H.Q. KANSAS FARM. No 1 Battery at YATTA HOUSE, A Section at BELLEVUE, B Section at WALLEMOLEN Reference map SPRIET 1/10000. Relief complete 3 O.R. Casualties. Transport, Stores & non attd: 25% personnel att: Hd Qrtrs Lines at DAMBRE	(6) 17
In the line	29th		Coy in the line. New battery position prepared at VIRILE FARM. (Authorise: the 1/10000 SPRIET) in preparation for coming attack.	(7) 17

Army Form C. 2118.

WAR DIARY
INTELLIGENCE SUMMARY.
(Erase heading not required.)

Instructions regarding War Diaries and Intelligence Summaries are contained in F. S. Regs., Part II. and the Staff Manual respectively. Title pages will be prepared in manuscript.

Place	Date	Hour	Summary of Events and Information	Remarks and references to Appendices
On the line	Nov 30th		Detachments in the line relieved by detachments from DAMBRE Camps. S.O.S. went up on our front at 7 a.m., Company's guns fired 26,000 rounds in response. at 5 p.m. all guns moved forward to new positions at VIRILE FARM. Lieut D. GARDINER slightly wounded	6/187 a.J. 7th March for O/c. 96th Coy M.G.C.

Army Form C. 2118.

WAR DIARY
or
INTELLIGENCE SUMMARY.
(Erase heading not required.)

War Diary.
96 Machine Gun Company.

Volume XXII

H. Williams Capt'
Cmd 96 M.G.Coy

WAR DIARY or INTELLIGENCE SUMMARY

Army Form C. 2118.

December 1917

Place	Date	Hour	Summary of Events and Information	Remarks and references to Appendices
LINE, Coy H.Q. KRONPRINZ FM. (Ref. map SPRIET 18,000)	1.		16 guns in position at VIRILE FM. (Ref map SPRIET 1/10,000). LT. D SARDINER wounded.	
	2	1.30a	Zero Hour for our Infantry. Attack did not develop, and Coy 16 guns had to remain at VIRILE FM. / 1.25.00 pm an harassing / Enemy Shelling. 2/LT. GRIFFITHS wounded; 3.O.R. KILLED and several wounded. SGT. MIDDLEMASS and PTE. SHORT gained M.M. Jn duration	
		4 p.m	to duty under heavy shell fire. 2/LT. C.S. GRUNDY from Reserve to U.K.	
		6 p.m	Weak enemy attack easily repulsed.	
	3		Reorganisation of guns to strengthen posn. 15 O.R. killed and wounded. Chiefly by snipping Coy withdrew from the line. 8 Guns were blown up at post with wounded and killed men. Coy marched to billets at DAMBRE CAMP.	
		6 p.m		(Ref map BELGIUM 28 N.W. 20,000)
DAMBRE CAMP Ref map BELGIUM 28 N.W.	4th — 9th		Coy in rest. Refitted. Gun Stores Completed. Reorganisation and Company Training. (6th) Major J.O.COOK from No 3 School, CAMIERS. 2/LT. L.H. SMITH on leave to U.K. (7th) 2/LT. L.H. STEPHENS from M.G. BASE. (8th) Major J.O. Cook to Command 182 M.G. Coy	
				20,000
9 HL LINE Coy H.Q. at HUBNER FM. (Ref. map POELCAPPELLE) Transport at DAMBRE CAMP	10th		Coy relieved 2 Guns 14 M.S. Coy at WALKEMOLEN (Ref. map SPRIET 10,000) 2 at TOURNANT FM. (Sound map) 4 " 215 M.S. Coy at BANFF H.Q. (Ronan Div. See Side Slip 1. 265H) BURNS H.Q. and Remaining Coy guns were put in in two sections for Defence in Depth. Weather very severe. Relief completed by 9 p.m. with no casualties	

WAR DIARY or INTELLIGENCE SUMMARY

Army Form C. 2118.

Place	Date Nov/17	Hour	Summary of Events and Information	Remarks and references to Appendices
LINE. (a) HQ at HUBNER FM (Rof Mop POELCAPPELLE)	11th	—	CAPT. WILLIAMS on leave to U.K. LT. J.B. NEILSON assuming temp'y command of Coy. Coy. Guns arranged as follows :— (a) FRONT LINE DEFENCE (as 6) BOHNE HO. — TOURNANT FM (b) SUPPORT (c) (d) DIVISIONAL LINE OF DEFENCE (BURNS HO. — VANHEULE FM. — WALLEMOLEN) (e) (f) CORPS LINE OF DEFENCE (Ref to Map SPRIET 1.8000) at WALLEMOLEN (Ref Map SPRIET). 1 Gun arranged at	
"	12th		Line Hutting. A Quiet Tour with only 30 R Casualties. Weather Very Severe, and Conditions of new Emplacements very difficult. (12 of these were made). 125,000 S.A.A. handed up to new positions. Harassing fire carried out on 16th and 17th, on all goods in (12th) LT. D. GARDINER reported Company from a C.C.S. (14th) LT D GARDINER on leave to U.K. (17th) LT J.B. NEILSON apptd 2.I.C. of the Company.	
LINE — DAMBRE CAMP. (Ref Map BELGIUM 28. N.W)	18th	10am to 6pm	Coy. relieved in the line by 97th M.G.Coy. Relief Co. pletes by 7.30 p.m without casualties. On relief Coy. travelled by train to billets in DAMBRE CAMP.	

Army Form C. 2118.

WAR DIARY
or
INTELLIGENCE SUMMARY.
(Erase heading not required.)

Instructions regarding War Diaries and Intelligence Summaries are contained in F. S. Regs., Part II. and the Staff Manual respectively. Title pages will be prepared in manuscript.

Place	Date	Hour	Summary of Events and Information	Remarks and references to Appendices
DAMBRE CAMP. Ref Map BELGIUM 28 N.W	Dec 19/17 to 23rd		Coy in prep. Reorganisation and Training. (20th) Baths, (21st) 2/Lt. SMITH proc. Leave to U.K.	
	24th	9.30am	"B" Sectn relieved guns of 14th and 97th M.G. Coys at GENOA F.M. and VON TIRPITZ F.M. (Rly Met POELCAPPELLE 10,000.)	
		3pm	Coy (Less B Sectn & Transport) relieved 14th M.G. Cy in Divl Support at CANAL BANK (Rly Met BELGIUM 28 N.W. 20,000) Transport (Less B. fighting Echelon) remain at DAMBRE CAMP.	
CANAL BANK.	25th to 29th		Coy (Less B Sectn) in Divl Support at CANAL BANK. Little training possible owing to lack of training ground, and the very severe weather, but Physical Drill, T.A. and Musketorn carried out daily. (27th) Capt. WILLIAMS received Command of Coy on return from leave to U.K.	
		8 am (29th)	"B" Sectn relieved in the line by Sectn of 219 M.G. Coy. Relief complete by 11 a.m. with no casualties.	

Army Form C. 2118.

WAR DIARY
or
INTELLIGENCE SUMMARY.
(Erase heading not required.)

Place	Date	Hour	Summary of Events and Information	Remarks and references to Appendices
CANAL BANK	30	11 am	2/Lt FRESHWATER on leave to U.K. Coy relieved by 117 Coy. (39th Division) Coy bussed by motor from ELVER-DINSE to AUDRUICQ (R/head HAZEBROUCK 1.30 am) the remainder to road billets at LE HAMEL and CLERQUES. Ref Scheme Move also CALAIS 10.00 am	[initials]
LE HAMEL CLERQUES R/Head HAZEBROUCK 5A.			Transport moved by road on same day from DAMBRE CAMP (reached CLERQUES 1/1/18).	
CALAIS	31.		Coy in rest. Cleaning up and refitment of billets.	

H. Williams Capt.
Comd. 96 M.G.Coy

WAR DIARY
or
INTELLIGENCE SUMMARY.

Army Form C. 2118.

96 Machine Gun Company
War Diary
Volume XXIII

WAR DIARY
INTELLIGENCE SUMMARY
(Erase heading not required.)

Army Form C. 2118.

Instructions regarding War Diaries and Intelligence Summaries are contained in F. S. Regs., Part II. and the Staff Manual respectively. Title pages will be prepared in manuscript.

Place	Date 1918	Hour	Summary of Events and Information	Remarks and references to Appendices
RECQUES AREA	May 1st	9-9.30am 10.15-10.45am 11.15-12.30	Physical training. Arms drill. Gun drill.	a)
	2nd	-do-	do for 1st inst.	a)
	3rd	-do-	do for 1st inst.	a)
	4th	-do- 2-3pm	do for 1st inst. Cleaning of gun stores & inspection of clothing.	a)
	5th		Holiday in lieu of Christmas Day. Football match in morning. Conversed with Lieut D. GARDINER returned from leave.	a)
	6th	Forenoon	Physical training, arms drill & stoppages. Lieut. J.B. NEILSON awarded the Military Cross - New Years Honours list. We & E/T/A's went to Calais to U.K.	a)
	7th	Forenoon	Physical training & arms drill. Special classes of instruction for Junior N.C.O's & Specialist men, the latter under 2/Lt. C.S. GRUNDY. commenced to day & were to carry on his further orders. G.O.C. 51st Division to Coy.	a)
	8th	Forenoon Afternoon	Gun work in billets owing to inclement weather. Lecture for N.C.Os	a)
	9th	Forenoon	Physical training & firing on the Range. Lieut. W.P. BROOMAN taken on strength of Coy.	a)

WAR DIARY
INTELLIGENCE SUMMARY.
(Erase heading not required.)

Army Form C. 2118.

Place	Date 1918	Hour	Summary of Events and Information	Remarks and references to Appendices
RECQUES Area	Jan 10th	Forenoon Afternoon	Physical training training. Firing on the range. Lecture for NCOs, into Section Leading all ranks	a).67
	11th	Forenoon Afternoon	Physical training - Firing on range. Recreational training & Lecture for NCOs. Inter Battery football match. No 2 Batty. 2 goals. No 1 Batty - nie	a).67
	12th	Forenoon	Physical training & Quipee tactical scheme	a).67
	13th	Forenoon Afternoon	All men of No. 1 Sec. Baths & change of underclothing Lecture for NCOs	a).67
	13th	Forenoon Afternoon	Physical training, arms drill, gun work in billets Lecture for NCOs.	a).67
	15th	Forenoon Afternoon	Physical training, arms drill + firing on range Lecture for NCOs. 2/Lt A.J.C FRESHWATER rejoined from leave	a).67
	16th	Forenoon	Physical training, arms drill, gun drill	a).67
	17th	Forenoon	Physical training, gun work in billets	a).67
	18th	Forenoon Afternoon	Physical training, arms drill. Transport left for forward area. Final lecture for NCOs	a).67

WAR DIARY
INTELLIGENCE SUMMARY

Army Form C. 2118.

Instructions regarding War Diaries and Intelligence Summaries are contained in F.S. Regs., Part II. and the Staff Manual respectively. Title pages will be prepared in manuscript.

Place	Date 1918	Hour	Summary of Events and Information	Remarks and references to Appendices
RECQUES AREA	Jan 19th		Company marches to AUDRICQ, thence by train to ELVERDINGE, then marches into Camp at HOSPITAL FARM	a)1.7
HOSPITAL FARM B.19.d.2.2.	20th	Forenoon	Physical training, Church Services, settling into Camp.	a)1.7
-do-	21st	Forenoon	Physical training & arms drill. 2/Lt STEPHEN'S went on leave to UK	a)1.7
-do-	22nd		Company moved from HOSPITAL FARM to CANAL BANK	a)1.7
CANAL BANK C.25.a.8.0.	23rd		Cleaning & improving dug outs & duckboards. Lieut Mr. G. ELIAS returned from leave to UK	a)1.7
-do-	24th	Forenoon	Physical training, arms drill, gun work	a)1.7
-do-	25th		Company moved to AMBROSE Camp in BOESINGHE area	a)1.7
AMBROSE CAMP B.10.d.central	26th		Physical training, arms drill, gun drill. Packing up, preparation for moving into the line tomorrow	a)1.7
-do-	27th		Physical training & Church Services. 8 guns moved into the line in the HOUTHULST WOOD Sector, relieving Hqrs of SIGNAL FARM U.21.c.2.0. relieving 53rd M.G. Coy.	a)1.7
-do-	28th		Physical training & arms drill. Packing up & preparation for moving into the line tomorrow.	a)1.7
SIGNAL FARM U.21.C.2.0	29th/31		Remainder of company moved into line in HOUTHULST FOREST Sector on 29th. Coy Headquarters SIGNAL FARM U.21.C.2.0. Owing to muddy weather observation difficult or impossible. Line quiet.	a)1.7

a)&b)1.7 for O.C. 96 M.G.

Copy No 1.

96th M.G. Coy. Relief Order No 30

Ref: SPRIET 1/10.000
     ZONNEBEKE 1/10.000

1. The 96th M.G. Coy is relieving the 97th M.G. Coy in the line on Nov 28th during the night Nov 28/29.

2. The Guns are distributed as follows:-
   8 Guns at the BATTERY taken over by No.2 Batt.
   1 Gun at VENTURE Fm   "   "   " " " "
   3 Guns at BELLE VUE   "   "   " " " "
   2 Guns at WALLEMOLEN   "   "   " " " "
   2 Guns at WOLF HOUSE   "   "   " " " "

3. Composition of the Batteries will be the following:-
   No.1 Bty. Lt. ...., 1 Sgt., ... Batman
   At VENTURE Fm   1 N.C.O. + 3 men
   " BELLE VUE   1 N.C.O. + 8 "
   " WOLF HOUSE   1 N.C.O. + 6 "
   " WALLEMOLEN   1 N.C.O. + 6 "

   No.2 Bty. Lt. NELSON, 1 Sgt., Batman, 2 O.R.

4. H.Q. orderlies will be attached as follows:
   Coy H.Q. ..... C.O's Orderly + 3 orderlies
   No.1 Bty ..... 2 orderlies
   No.2 Bty ..... 1 orderly

5. Batteries for the line will parade at 7.15 am ready to march off. H.Q. orderlies will report to the Bty to which they are attached.

6. Dress:- Battle order, leather jerkins

7. Three days rations and the iron ration will be taken.

8. Lorries will convey all ranks to KANSAS CROSS whence they will proceed to HAVEN POST where point guides will take them to their respective positions.

Relieving team for VENTURE PM will wait at KANSAS PM until dusk.

9. Administrative details have been communicated to all concerned.

10. PLEASE ACKNOWLEDGE

Issued at 6 p.m.

H. Williams Capt,
Commdg 96th M. G. Coy

Copies to :-
    1+2. War Diary
    3. Field
    4. O.C.
    5. O.C. 31st Bty
    6. O.C. No. 2 Coy
    7. Lt GARDNER
    8. Lt NEILSON
    9. Lt FRESHWATER
    10. C.S.M.
    11. 96th Coy. Bde.
    12. O.C. 97th M. G. Coy

"C" Coy Operation Order No. 5.

1. No. 5 Bty 96 M.G. Coy is relieving 8 guns of 55 M.G. Coy in the line on the night Jan 29th/30th.

2. Guns to be taken over are numbered 1-8 from right to left.

3. Bty H.Q. will be at FORT HQ

4. Tripods & belt boxes will be taken over in the line, also all maps, defence schemes targets & calculations.

5. Relief complete & all reports will be sent to SIGNAL FM which will be Coy H.Q.

6. Guides will be at SIGNAL FM at 4 pm. to guide teams & limbers to their respective positions. N.C.Os must know the number of the guns they are relieving

7. Two limbers will be placed at the disposal of OC No 2 Bty to convey guns etc to the line.

8. Please acknowledge.

H H Williams Capt.

Copies to:-
1. O.C.
2. O.C. No 1 Bty
3. O.C. No 2 Bty
4. Adjt & Cmdt
5. I.O.

6.
7. BMGO
8. 54 M.G. Coy
9. File
10. War Diary

Copy No. 16

H. M.G. Coy Operation Order No 37

1. No. 1 B/y H. M.G. Coy is relieving 8 guns of 53rd M.G. Coy in the line tomorrow Jan 27th 1918.

2. Guns to be taken over are divided as follows:
    2 Guns at PASCAL P.M.
    2 "   " JEW BEND
    2 "   " JAPAN HQ
    2 "   " GRUYTERS2..??..P..

3. The B/y Commander will have his HQ at SIGNAL P.M. and his second officer at PASCAL P.M.
   Details of personnel have been communicated to Officers concerned.

4. Tripods & belt boxes will be taken over in the line, and all notes, defense schemes, targets, & calculations.

5. Guides will be at SIGNAL P.M. at 11.30 AM to take teams to their respective positions. N.C.Os should know the names of the positions to which they are going.

No. 96 MACHINE GUN COMPANY.
No. 11
Date 16.7.17

96th M.G. Coy Relief Orders

(1) The 96th M.G. Coy is being relieved by the 146th M.G. Coy on the night 19th/20 July.

(2) Groups will be relieved as follows:-
No I Group by "B" Section 146 M.G.C. + ½ "D" Section
No II "   " "A"   "   "   "   + ½ "   "
No III Group - "C"   "   "   "

(3) Tripods, belt boxes (8 per gun) trench mountings and S.A.A. will be handed over; also all maps, range charts and defence schemes. Receipts will be given and received.

(4) 146th M.G. Coy will send one officer and 1 N.C.O. or m. per gun into the line on the night of the 18th/19th. Group Commanders will ensure that these men know thoroughly the part played in the defence scheme by their respective guns.

(5) The sections of incoming Company will be taken from Company H.Q. by H.Q. guides up to their respective Group H.Q. Arrived there each gun team will be met by its own guide from the party mentioned in para 4.

(6) Times of Arrival of incoming sections at Coy H.Q. will be as follows:-
"C" Section   9 P.M.
"B"   "   9.15 P.M.
"A"   "   9.30 "

Should the day be dull and cloudy these sections may be expected to arrive rather earlier. Group Commanders will arrange, therefore, to have (cont) the team guides of 146th M.G. Coy at their H.Q. in good time, so that the relief may not be delayed.

(6) H.Q. limber 96th M.G.Coy will report at Coy H.Q. at 9.30 p.m. Three fighting limbers 16th M.G.Coy will be at Coy H.Q. at 11.15p.m., 11.30 p.m. respectively.

(7) On relief Sections will proceed to Coy H.Q. report arrival, pack limbers, & proceed to billets in JEANNIOL CAMP CORPAE, where a meal will be provided for them.

(8) ACKNOWLEDGE.

H. Williams Captain
Commanding 16th M.G.Coy

Issued at

Copies to:-
1) O.C. 96th M.G.Coy
2) O.C. No1 Group
3) "   "   "2   "
4) "   "   "3   "
5) 2nd I/C 16th M.G.Coy
6) Transport Officer
7) 96th Inf. Bde
8) D.M.G.O. 32nd Divn.
9) O.C. 146th M.G.Coy.
10) War Diary
11) "   "
12) File.

Army Form C. 2118.

WAR DIARY
or
INTELLIGENCE SUMMARY
(Erase heading not required.)

WA 24

War Diary
96th M.G. Coy
Vol. No. XXIV
February 1918

H. Williams Capt
Comd 96 M.G. Coy

Army Form C. 2118

WAR DIARY
or
INTELLIGENCE SUMMARY
(Erase heading not required.)

Instructions regarding War Diaries and Intelligence Summaries are contained in F. S. Regs., Part II. and the Staff Manual respectively. Title Pages will be prepared in manuscript.

Place	Date	Hour	Summary of Events and Information	Remarks and references to Appendices
HOUTHULST FOREST SECTOR	7th 1/7/17		Company in the line. Continual Retaliation on Enemy machine Gun fire, about 4,000 rounds daily. Coy. H.Q. at Signal Farm.	1/8
MARGUERITE CAMP	8th		Company relieved in the line, excepting two guns, by 14th Br. G. Coy. & marched down to MARGUERITE CAMP B.9.c.1.9	1/9
-do-	9th		Day spent in cleaning up & refitting & resting.	1/9
-do-	10th		Forenoon Physical Training & ammo drive. Afternoon Smoke Parties.	
DEKORT CAMP	11th		Coy. moved to DEKORT CAMP B.3.a.5.5. In afternoon 8 guns relieved the guns of 97th M.G. Coy. & put an extra one in the line about W.16 b. 10.15. Coy. H.Q. at SIGNAL FARM	1/10
HOUTHULST FOREST SECTOR	12/17		No firing done.	

Army Form C. 2118.

WAR DIARY
or
INTELLIGENCE SUMMARY
(Erase heading not required.)

Place	Date	Hour	Summary of Events and Information	Remarks and references to Appendices
HOULTHULST FOREST SECTOR	Feb 18		In afternoon 4 extra guns were sent to the line to LOUVOIS FARM U.11.a central to barrage fire during an extensive raid along the Divisional front at night. These guns together with the other guns in the line fired 50,000 rounds. The raid was successful, commenced at 11 P.M.	110
— do —	19/20		Things quiet in the line, did no firing	
— do —	21st		Company ceases to exist as a separate unit & from this day forms part of the 32nd Divn M.G. Batt.	116

Lt. Williams Cpt.
Com'd 96 M.G. Coy